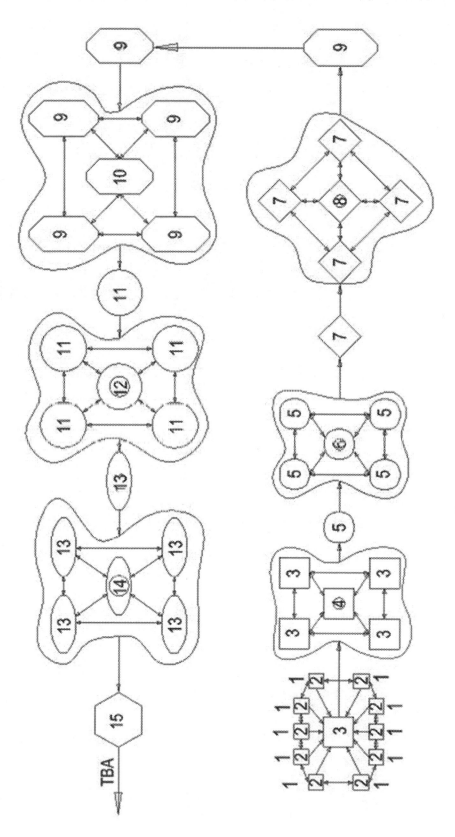

FAMILY CELL= 1   PRIVATE HUB= 2   PRIVATE STRATUM= 3   NEIGHBORHOOD HUB= 4

NEIGHBORHOOD STRATUM= 5   COMMUNITY HUB= 6   COMMUNITY STRATUM= 7   SOCIAL HUB= 8

SOCIAL STRATUM= 9   INDUSTRIAL HUB= 10   INDUSTRIAL STRATUM= 11   NATIONAL HUB= 12

NATIONAL STRATUM= 13   UNIVERSAL HUB= 14   UNIVERSAL STRATUM= 15   HIGHER LEVEL IF ANY= TBA

Socio-Cultural Harmonic Human Settlements and Urbanization

NADIM AHMED

authorHOUSE®

AuthorHouse™
1663 Liberty Drive
Bloomington, IN 47403
www.authorhouse.com
Phone: 1 (800) 839-8640

Published by AuthorHouse   11/24/2015

ISBN: 978-1-5049-5834-9 (sc)
ISBN: 978-1-5049-5833-2 (e)

Library of Congress Control Number: 2015917667

Print information available on the last page.

Any people depicted in stock imagery provided by Thinkstock are models, and such images are being used for illustrative purposes only. Certain stock imagery © Thinkstock.

This book is printed on acid-free paper.

Because of the dynamic nature of the Internet, any web addresses or links contained in this book may have changed since publication and may no longer be valid. The views expressed in this work are solely those of the author and do not necessarily reflect the views of the publisher, and the publisher hereby disclaims any responsibility for them.

(snahmed129@yahoo.com, nadimahmeds@ymail.com)

INTELLECTUAL PROPERTY
DECLARATION

This is to inform the readers and all those concerned that the work declared here in this book is the original work, creation of the mind and intellectual property of the author, Mr. Nadim Ahmed, and cannot be used, applied, implied or referenced and implemented spatially or in any means and for any purpose without the prior permission of the author. All those found in the thefting of the idea mentioned in this book would be prosecuted in the International court of law, the court of law in USA and if required also in the country where breach of this intellectual property occurs. Organizations, agencies, companies, communities, authorities, states and governments etc., who have interest in applying the idea of Socio-Cultural Harmonic Human Settlements and Urbanization, must in advance seek written permission from the author and the intellectual property owner of this idea through the contacts as mentioned in this book

DEDICATION

I dedicate this work in Socio-Cultural Harmonic Human Settlements and Urbanization and related book to my wife and children who encouraged and inspired me during my research work and in compilation of this work in the form of a book. I would also like to dedicate this book to my mother and father whose continuous efforts towards my education and social training made me capable to do years of research and also in the writing of this book

CONTENTS

Intellectual Property Declaration..v

Dedication vii

Preface xi

Introduction..xiii

Society And Urbanization 1

Contemporary Human Settlements And Urbanization...8

Socio-Cultural Harmonic Human Settlements And Urabanization 12

Socio-Cultural Harmonic Transportation Systems 50

Formulation Of The Principles 75

References 81

PREFACE

Settlements of human beings mean the totality of the human community with all the social and cultural elements that sustain it and maintain it. Therefore, instead of structural spatial landscapes, the human settlements should be seen as the social and cultural landscapes that developed over time. Furthermore, due to processes of urban sprawl all over the world, the existing classification between the urban and the rural is losing importance, and this point of view is already represented by contemporary planning strategies. Hence, an integrative geography of settlements that considers urban and rural settlements as a continuum of cultural and social landscapes is required in order to get solution to many issues contemporary human settlements are facing in urban areas

An approach in this direction is a subjective formula for the development of human settlements, urban areas and related infrastructures that include the classification of social activities based on their social activity types and energy levels; creation and classification of hubs of human social activities and then allocation of the above mentioned classified social activities to such hubs of social activities towards the accomplishment of goals and objectives of lives of individual human beings with the help of collective efforts of fellow human beings; and uniform and harmonic distribution of such social activity hubs such that social hubs with lower social activity energy levels and types encircle the corresponding hub with higher social activity energy levels and types, which in turn encircle the corresponding hub with further higher social activity energy levels and types and so on, with human settlements, in residential units and houses, built around the human social activity hub with comparatively lowest level human social activity energy and related types only. Such classification includes all aspects of a society, its essential components and related activities for an optimal outcome to bring happiness and enjoyment to individuals for which they entered into the social contract along with their fellow beings. When we talk about enjoyment of fruits of individual efforts then this is essential that there be spatial arrangements for such roles to play. Early human settlements in records show such arrangements where the family meant extended or secondary families living together or nearby with a common meetup place for all these related families so that they may in their physical and spiritual connections achieve happiness-the ultimate goal of human living in the relation to each other, because human beings in commonality of language, culture and blood relations have such spiritual connections with each other developed over the years of communications and physical presence in all occasions with relation to the land with all of its physical and material as well as spiritual expressions. Hence the dream of happiness and joy from the fruits of individual achievements cannot be fulfilled without a strong and durable relationship of man with the land, families, relatives and friends, which could only be possible through man's long term direct and intimate connections with these factors spanning over life. Industries and financial organizations have to be brought optimally and feasibly closer to these settlements in harmonic and uniform fashion within logical distances instead of men being forced to break the chains of such valuable and important social links and migrate and mobilize to serve these industries and financial setups

INTRODUCTION

Human beings are social beings but at the same time they need privacy as well as family life. Human beings need each other to support each other emotionally, socially, morally, financially and professionally to prosper as an individual as well as a group. The various dynamics of a human society urge human beings to live together so that they may benefit and support each other for their existence and achievement of personal goals and objectives of lives but at the same time, they need to have periods of isolation and self-containment to enjoy the fruits of their achievements and be happy. This is an ideal that a society should be built upon spatially, this was the reason a society came into being and this must be the basis of human settlements and urban planning. Human beings have spiritual connections and this connection grows stronger with the amount of time and years spent together in direct, intimate and physical presence and communications as families, relations, neighbors and friends etc. The ultimate goal of human living is happiness and enjoyment of individual achievements and this could only be achieved by sharing and celebrating it with those with whom the respective man has strong physical and spiritual connections such as primary and secondary families, close relations, neighbors and friends etc. This is essential in the building of human settlements and urban dwellings and related infrastructure to bring happiness and joy to the members of a society

Now furthermore, if the infrastructure of an urban society is uniform and harmonic in its manifestation, then each and every setup and related social activities would be predictable and hence the behavior of human beings living therein. This would greatly reduce the energy losses as well as the time losses because of optimal everyday mass movement of human beings and related accessories and would greatly increase the probability of uniform resource distribution among its dwellers without getting into various issues contemporary urbanization is facing such as alienation, stress, increased daily life costs, and negative social aspects that result from mass marginalization. This can be achieved through the approach in urban planning as mentioned below:

This method of development of human settlements and urbanizations and related infrastructure, hereby called Socio-Cultural Harmonic Human Settlements and Urbanization or Social Activity Energy Classified Galaxial Human Settlements and Urbanization, is a comprehensive and logically derived invention into latest and up to date trends and developments in this area of human settlements and urbanization with vision into the future and are unique, original, inventive, never perceived and never used before. As human beings have unlimited desires but limited resources in terms of material, time and skills and thus needed other human beings to work together towards the achievement of individual goals and fulfillment of desires, thus societies were formed, where man started to live in families and relations thus developing clusters of dwellings which in turn transformed into neighborhoods. As human population grew, neighborhoods combined together and formed communities, which then formed logical boundaries of societies. Scientific advancements and invention of currencies made this possible for man to produce and exchange goods and other commodities in huge quantities to fulfill the human desires and accomplish goals. This gave rise to large numbers of production and commercial centers to produce and trade commodities and other products

At this point in history, human dwellings became vast and societies, as smaller human dwellings grew into huge urban centers, lost their meaning of being societies and the very essential and basic components such as family compounds, neighborhoods or mohallas and their logical and harmonic and uniform orientation in space. All necessary and integral components got mixed up in disorderly manners thus causing tremendous amount of energies wasted as well as the fabric of human to human and human to nature relations torn apart causing human beings denied happiness and caused various types of psychological and mental pain and stresses. The Industrialization progress and developments in 19th and 20th centuries were controlled by capitalists, and urban planners either planned cities and urban areas as per the viewpoint of capitalists and industrialists or they were not able to present a solution to this issue. Hence an optimal approach is required which may satisfy capitalists and industrialists as well as the inhabitants of such urban sprawls and domains

Socio-Cultural Harmonic Urban Planning can solve this issue, because this type of urban planning is based on social and cultural aspects and elements of human living, and recommends and suggests establishment of Family Domains, Neighborhood Domains, Community Domains, Social Domains, Industrial Domains etc in an harmonic fashion without disturbing or interfering into each other's domains and purpose thus forming a harmonized and very logical distribution of social activities hubs based on types and social activity energy levels. Urban Planners did not pay much attention to the application of the basic principles on which man established societies. As urban domain is the action ground of societies, therefore, an urban area must be created based on the basic principles of a society--All a man does is the Social Activity thus an Urban Area is the spatial domain to perform this social activity; Each and every social activity has a specific type or related required social energy level- Hence all social activities must be classified based on the above mentioned principle; These classified social activities must be assigned to specific Social Activity Hubs; These Hubs must be placed spatially in an harmonic fashion so that no 2 Hubs can interfere into each others domain. This is the only way we can formulate or (and) create an urban settlement with optimal and efficient social energy consumption by the dwellers without causing all the contemporary problems and issues urban settlements are facing nowadays

SOCIETY AND URBANIZATION

The present day cities have been developed consciously or unconsciously in a manner to suit capitalism and industrialization and also the rapid mass labor mobilization to work places at a minimum cost to the industrialist and capitalists. This is the reason no serious and sincere efforts were ever made to create a socio-cultural urban environment. Contemporary urban developments are such that they cost tremendous amount of mental and physical energy to the dwellers to mobilize within these urban dwellings and find places of social activities, facilities and amenities in addition to the stresses they have to go through both mentally and physically. Huge highways have been built with millions of cars and vehicles speeding around for mobilization of masses used 90% of times for back and forth movement of labors, workers and professionals to work places and their respective residences, and all these energies and resources for mobilization are at the expense of the masses. The more they built highways, speedways, expressways, super ways, the more the traffic problems and congestions and sufferings for the travelers spending hours on these highways and super ways. Urban planners from time to time brought in many ideas and implemented them to solve such issues such as Garden Movement, New Urbanism, Unified Settlement Planning, Landscape Urbanism etc. Latest innovation is Mixed-Use Developments to solve mobilization issues, but each and every innovation at one place solved some issues and created another. For example, take the Mixed-Use Development claims to solve the mass mobilization issue. But contrary to their claims, I have seen these developments where people reside but instead of working within such developments they work in previously established Industrial-Zones thus further creating the issue of traffic congestion and creating other social issues such as privacy issues, more crimes and insecurity, higher stress, lack of play grounds, lack of space, daylight etc. A building or such development cannot have all the facilities, and therefore, their claim of providing ease of availability of social amenities and facilities is not a reality as they have to go from building to building facing accessibility issues etc

When man established societies, came with it a strong bonding relationship with the land because this was the pre-requisite or requirement for a society to come into being. People had been living in the same place for generations. Industrialization broke this bonding as more and more workers, labors and professionals were required irrespective of their nationalities and gender. Family bondings were not desirable either, therefore, an urban infra-structure was required where emotionless human beings could reside as commodities and may be utilized to fed the industries and commercial and trade centers. Huge buildings, mixed-use residential towers and complexes were ideal for such purpose. The purpose was twofold- Provide human materials to the industries, factories, service centers, commercial and financial institutes and trade zones and force the subjects to buy or rent residential units at a very elevated cost to further the financial benefits of capitalist classes. This was also important to separate the wives and husbands, so that they may not be able spend much energy towards family developments and nurturing so that most of their energies may be utilized to the benefits of such production and service centers. Due to breakup or weakening of family bondings, many social and emotional issues evolved out of human behavior and attitude towards self and other fellow beings. This is the time now to pause, evaluate and analyze our approach and direction and correct the path and direction to optimize human efforts and achievements to avoid further damage to humanity. This is, therefore, needed to come up with an urban plan which may provide an optimal solution for all the stake holders of urban living without the cost of their family living and alienation issues, stresses, increased daily life costs, and negative social aspects that result from mass marginalization of the dwellers of such urbanization and human settlements

Such an approach is required now, when democratic governments are becoming more and more citizen welfare oriented and common masses are getting more say in the everyday and policy matters of their governments, where an urban plan may be envisaged and formulated which will return much of the lost family living and related happiness, so that instead of being the tools for capitalization and industrialization, masses may become able to materialize the very reasons for which they agreed to a social setup where they could live together thousands of years ago, in order to enjoy the fruits of their individual achievements with the help of the collective efforts of their fellow beings

Hence we can say that **urban planning** or **city** or **town planning** has to be a technical, social, cultural and political process related to the use of land and design of the urban environment and infrastructure including transportation networks etc, based on socio-cultural traits and characteristics of human living, to guide and ensure the orderly development of human settlements and communities. It should also concerns itself with research and analysis and strategic thinking to achieve a socio-cultural spatial representation of a uniform and harmonic distribution of social activity hubs and facilities centers to minimize energy losses, stresses, alienation and negative social impacts and maximize happiness, social and cultural interaction, quality family living and time to enjoy fruits of individual achievements with family, relatives and friends

For this purpose we have to go back in time to the point where we may find the very basic principles and components of the formation of a society when man was happy enough by making collective efforts with fellow human beings to achieve individual goals and enjoying the fruits of individual achievements in the places of solitude with his family, relatives and friends. Therefore, we need to understand the basic definitions of some very common terminologies we use in our daily social living related to human settlements and urbanization specifically

Society is a group of people sharing the same geographical territory and therefore subject to the same political authority and dominant cultural expectations. Such people share a distinctive culture and institutions, which characterize the patterns of social relations between them. Large societies typically further develop social stratification and dominance patterns among its subgroups. A given society may be described as sum of social relationships among its members

Human beings had been living in hunter-gatherer societies for millions of years. The hunter gatherer society did not practice agriculture and used to raise and herd animals. Social structure was usually egalitarian with little economic and gender inequality. Private property was minimal and they had no settled area on land for permanent housings. In a hunter-gatherer society the primary subsistence method involves the direct procurement of edible plants and animals from the wild, foraging and hunting without significant recourse to the domestication of either. This was since the invention of agriculture, hunter-gathering society have been replaced by farming or pastoralist societies in most parts of the world and human beings begin to settle and started getting associated with land. Horticulture and agriculture as types of subsistence developed among humans somewhere between 10,000 and 8,000 years ago in the region of the fertile and climatically feasible Middle East

Agriculture allows a much greater density of population than can be supported by hunting and gathering and allows for the accumulation of excess product to keep for winter use or to sell for profit. The ability of farmers to feed large numbers of people whose activities have nothing to do with material production was the crucial factor in the rise of surplus, specialization, advanced technology, hierarchical social structures, inequality, and standing armies. Agrarian societies thus support the emergence of a more complex social structure. It is when the concept of building houses and residential structures started. Man learned to build cluster of residential units close together and surrounded the farmlands and work places and a clear concept of Family structures evolved alongwith relation to land. Agrarian societies led to the introduction of property rights, patriarchal social setup, domestication of plants and animals, and larger families. It was around such time period when the society was transformed and State was formed assumed to be founded on Social Contract

In moral and political philosophy, the **social contract** or **political contract** is a theory or model, originating during the Age of Enlightenment, that typically addresses the questions of the origin of society and the legitimacy of the authority of the state over the individual. Social contract arguments, as suggested by Thomas Hobbes and Jean Jacques Rousseau, typically posit that individuals have consented, either explicitly or tacitly, to surrender some or all of their freedoms and submit to the authority of the ruler or magistrate (or to the decision of a majority), in exchange for protection of their remaining rights. The question of the relation between natural and legal rights, therefore, is often an aspect of social contract theory. This led to the formation of societies

Family is the unit of socialization, a socially recognizable group in physical representation. One obvious sign of a family is that of a common residence, housing two or more persons related by birth, marriage, or adoption, who reside together. In addition, there is usually a long term commitment of the man and the woman, a joint economic goal, other shared goals and values, a socially approved relationship. The primary function of a family is that of reproducing society, the birth, nurture, training and education of children. This is called **Nuclear Family**. Families transformed into **Extended Families**, which refers to grandparents, aunts, uncles, and cousins. A strong relationship with extended families was socially as rewarding as close ties inside the nuclear family. Thus extended family also ensures the survival of the family members by providing the protective aspect of the "herd" instinct in human beings which provides safety of its members by polarizing into groups. This security also promotes sharing work and property, emotional support, and birth, growth and nurturing of children

The concept of the family, therefore, should be the most important part of our urbanization. This is basic building unit and any error in this respect means a complete erroneous, in-efficient and failed urban planning and corresponding urban development. As families grew in numbers, they started living in groups of relatives. Individual Nuclear Families and Extended Families functioned as part of groups in such a manner that their lives were greatly influenced by the group even more so than by their own individual beliefs. People spent more time together in such groups in both a physical sense and social as well. Of course, the most important group had always been the family, which encompassed a broad sense of kinship even among those family members living in separate residences. In order to perform such functions, the socializing space or place needed was called House. It is, therefore, the primary building block of a society physically and spatially. The houses built were usually such that they used to have a Central Meeting Place and living quarters for single and married were built around this Central Meeting Place with usually closed boundaries. Extended families might have been using the Central Meeting Place to socialize and spend quality time with each other and communicate to support each other socially and economically for a better and secured living. These houses were usually built around the agricultural lands. In addition to the financial and social security, such extended family and friends structure with its members in physical and direct presence and communications with each other over a long span of their lives create, develop, nurture and nourish a sense of physical and spiritual cohesiveness and attachment necessary for human beings to experience happiness and joy just by their being physically present which no other form of material and social achievement and success can bring into a human being. This is very important and in fact I would say the most important factor in the life of a person socially. In the struggle for material success and possession, man forgot this most important factor

Industrialization and capitalization weakened this most important connections between human beings, weakened the relation of man with the land, caused mass mobilization and migration, displacing millions and millions within and abroad their countries or native lands in search of happiness wrongly associated with material possessions and successes. Man for centuries established its relation with the lands and used to settle and live at a place for centuries with their children, grandchildren, grand grandchildren and so on, all living and growing up and spending their whole lives at the places of their forefathers. This essentially brought genetic changes into the brains of human beings and made them to feel happiness and joy associated with their nuclear and extended families and friends. All is lost during industrialization and globalization. This pattern of globalization and industrialization must be curtailed and minimized in order to bring back the much lost happiness, joy and pleasures man had in his connection with families nuclear and extended, friends and the land

Neighborhoods are common, and perhaps close to universal. A **neighborhood** should usually supposed to be a combination of many Nuclear or Extended Family houses built together in a close area or space and is a geographically localized community within a larger city, town, suburb or rural area. Neighborhoods are often social communities with considerable face-to-face interaction among members. It is generally defined spatially as a specific geographic area and functionally as a set of social networks. Neighborhoods, then, are the spatial units in which face-to-face social interactions occur—the personal settings and situations where residents seek to realize common values, socialize youth, and maintain effective social control while maintaining face-to-face communication. In a Neighborhood people are visible to each other as well as their social activities on daily basis including all in social hierarchy

In the words of the urban scholar Lewis Mumford, "Neighborhoods, in some primitive, inchoate fashion exist wherever human beings congregate, in permanent family dwellings; and many of the functions of the city tend to be distributed naturally". Most of the earliest cities around the world as excavated by archaeologists have evidence for the presence of social neighborhoods. Neighborhoods are typically generated by social interaction among people living near one another. In this sense they are local social units larger than households not under the control of city or state officials. The residents used to have connections and relations with the land and the people sharing the same place from generations and staying together for their whole life keeping associations with the land, culture, language and people

But in addition to these benefits, considerable research indicates that strong and cohesive neighborhoods and communities are linked—quite possibly causally linked—to decreases in crime, better outcomes for children, and improved physical and mental health. The social support that a strong neighborhood may provide can serve as a buffer. **Hence Neighborhoods should be considered as a semi-closed-boundary spatial representation of a society usually comprised of families, their relatives, close friends, close acquaintances and other socially and culturally related individuals and groups**. Trespassing and foreign movements and interference are usually not the norms of a Neighborhood. In Asia such dwellings have erected boundaries encompassing approximately 25 to 100 houses with all the required facilities and activities of social nature

Community is a group of interacting people sharing an environment in a common location. In human communities, intent, belief, resources, preferences, needs, risks, and a number of other conditions may be present in common, affecting the identity of the participants and their degree of cohesiveness, and need organization and order. Therefore, Community is often used to refer to a group that is, though may not be related, organized around common values and is attributed with social cohesion within a shared geographical location, generally in social units larger than a household and a neighborhood

People's perception of interconnection and interdependence, shared responsibility and common goals lead to the formation of a Community. A village was a very good example of a mixture of Neighborhood and Community where, although many patterns of village life have existed, the typical village was small, consisting of perhaps 25 to 30 families. Homes were situated together for sociability and defense, and land surrounding living quarters was farmed. German sociologist Ferdinand Tönnies distinguished between two types of human association: *Gemeinschaft* (usually translated as "community") and *Gesellschaft* ("society" or "association"). In his 1887 work, *Gemeinschaft und Gesellschaft*, Tönnies argued that *Gemeinschaft* is perceived to be a tighter and more cohesive social entity, due to the presence of a "unity of will". He added that family and kinship were the perfect expressions of *Gemeinschaft*, but that other shared characteristics, such as place or belief, could also result in *Gemeinschaft*. This paradigm of communal networks and shared social understanding has been applied to multiple cultures in many places in history. *Gesellschaft*, on other hand, is a group in which individuals who make up group are motivated to take part in the group purely by self or group interest

CONTEMPORARY HUMAN SETTLEMENTS AND URBANIZATION

During the Neolithic period, human societies underwent major cultural and economic changes, including transformation of hunter-and-gather to horticulture to the development of agriculture, the formation of sedentary societies and fixed settlements, increasing population densities, and the use of relatively advanced and more complex tools. Neolithic Revolution, has taken place independently multiple times in human history

Agrarian societies, with the industrial revolution in the West during 18th and 19th centuries, transformed significantly into industrial societies, which refers to a society driven by the use of technology to enable mass production, supporting a large population with a high capacity for division. Such a structure developed in the west in the period of time following the industrial revolution, and replaced the agrarian societies of the pre-modern, pre-industrial age. Industrial societies are generally mass societies, and may be succeeded in future by an Information society. Industrial society makes the urbanization desirable, in part so that workers can be closer to centers of production, and the service industry can provide labor to workers and those that benefit financially from them, in exchange for a share of production profits with which they can buy goods of their livelihood. This leads to the rise of very large cities and surrounding suburban areas with a high rate of economic activity. Mass society possesses a mass culture and large scale impersonal, social institutions. A mass society is a society in which prosperity and bureaucracy have weakened traditional social ties and aristocratic values

The impact of industrialization on family structures has been no less dramatic. The consequences for families can be seen in its changing functions, smaller size, altered composition, and changing roles of its members. In industrial societies, many of the family's traditional functions have been eliminated or greatly altered. The family is now an economic unit only in terms of consumption, not of production. Families no longer control political system. Schools, religious groups, and other organizations have assumed much of the responsibility for the education, socialization, and supervision of children etc

Urbanization is a rapid and historic transformation of human living on a global scale, whereby predominantly rural culture is being rapidly replaced by urban culture. The last major change in settlement patterns was the accumulation of hunter-gatherers into villages many thousand years ago hence giving rise to agrarian societies. This culture is characterized by the common blood lines, intimate relationships, and communal behavior whereas urban culture is characterized by distant bloodlines, unfamiliar relations, and competitive behavior. Till the 18th century the ratio of rural to urban population remained at a fixed equilibrium. With the onset of the agricultural and industrial revolution in the late 18th century this relationship was finally broken and an unprecedented growth in urban population took place over the course of the 19th century, both through continued migration from the countryside and due to the tremendous demographic expansions that occurred at that time

The modern origins of urban planning lie in the movement for urban reforms that arose as a reaction against the disorder of the cities in the mid-19th century. Urban planning can include urban renewal, by adapting urban planning techniques to existing cities suffering from decline. In the late 20th century, the term sustainable development has come to represent an ideal outcome in the sum of all planning goals

Urbanization occurs as individual, commercial, social and governmental efforts to reduce time and expense in commuting and transportation and improve opportunities for jobs, education, housing, and transportation. Living in cities permits the advantages of the opportunities of proximity, diversity, and marketplace competition. However, the advantages of urbanization are weighed against alienation issues, stress, increased daily life costs, and negative social aspects that result from mass marginalization. Also instead in fact todays huge expansion of urban settlements have caused much transportation oriented problems and commuters spend almost 3 to 5 hours on highways and roads on daily basis. Social amenities, facilities, places of socialization, meetup places, educational institutes etc are now far spread over an average radius of 35 to 50 Kilometers. Mass Transit systems are also under extreme pressure and loads in addition to environmental degradation it causes. In order to find solutions related to the contemporary problems and negative impacts of urbanization, urban theorists and planners have come up with various solutions. Few related to my work have been discussed here in brief as follows:

New Urbanism is an urban design movement which promotes use of walkable neighborhoods containing a range of housing and job types. It arose in the United States in the early 1980s, and has gradually transformed many aspects of real estate development, urban planning, and municipal land-use strategies. New Urbanism is strongly influenced by urban design standards that were prominent until the rise of the automobile in the mid-20th century; it encompasses principles such as traditional neighborhood design and transit-oriented development. It is also closely related to regionalism, environmentalism and the broader concept of smart growth. The movement also includes a more pedestrian-oriented variant known as New Pedestrianism, which has its origins in a 1929 planned community in Radburn, New Jersey. This urbanism is valuable and helps create a better Neighborhood and Community but cannot address many issues being faced by modern urban dwellers such as mass movement through highways and expressways, access to socialization and facilities centers, logical and optimal relationship between neighborhoods, communities and social centers and cultural aspects of the human spatial settlements etc

Unified Settlement Planning (USP) is the component of regional planning where a unified approach is applied for a region's overall development. Regions use their land for various settlement purposes including agriculture, manufacturing and public administration. For society to develop it has to amalgamate and develop settlements in which their coexistence is the basis for a holistic development of any society. Unified Settlement planning is a contemporary approach for the bulk requirement of urban amenities, for the vast regions of the developing countries with uniformly distributed human settlement patterns. The approach utilizes the advantages of the uniformly distributed human settlement patterns and avoids the difficulties caused by the dense network of roads and villages, all over the regions. Unified settlement planning allows holistic regional development without significantly disturbing existing villages, farmland, bodies of water, and forests

Landscape Urbanism is a theory of urban planning arguing that the best way to organize cities is through the design of the city's landscape, rather than the design of its buildings. The phrase 'Landscape Urbanism' first appeared in the mid 1990s in the work of Peter Connolly, a Masters of Urban Design student from RMIT Melbourne. Since this time, phrase 'Landscape Urbanism' has taken on many different uses and response to the failings of New Urbanism and the shift away from the comprehensive visions, and demands, for modern architecture and urban planning. In addition to these Downtown Concept, Pedestrian Urbanism, Garden City movement, Grid Systems etc were implemented in addition to the latest trend into Mixed-Use Urbanism

Till this date all approaches to solve the various issues contemporary urbanization is facing, have been able to address specific aspects of human settlements and living but have not been successful or could not achieve an optimal solution for all the major issues of human living in an urban settlement. The reason why all such efforts could not bring in the desired results, in my opinion, was the land management approach of urban planners. They could not consider urban planning as an application of human social behavior pattern or as an application of socio-cultural aspects of human living. Even if some did they could not realize and materialize this into spatial representation logically and effectively. Man is a social being and has a certain social pattern of behaviors manifested in its various approaches while interacting and communicating with each other as a society. The solution is in the simplicity of the earliest social setups man adapted and by researching those very basic foundation principles into the transformation of human settlements to industrialization and globalization from socio-cultural aspects. This way we can find the solution for many issues for our contemporary societies in urbanization

SOCIO-CULTURAL HARMONIC HUMAN SETTLEMENTS AND URABANIZATION

The term space has commonly been used in place of cultural landscape to describe landscapes that are "produced or mediated by human behavior to elicit certain behaviors". Defined in this manner, archaeologists, such as Delle, have theorized space as composed of three components: the material, social, and cognitive. Material space is any space that is created by people either through physical means or through the establishment of definitions, descriptions and rules of what a space is reserved for and how it should be used (Delle). Social space is what dictates a person's relationship with others and the material space (Delle). Social space is how one uses their material space to interact with others and navigate throughout their world. Cognitive space is how people comprehend their social and material spaces—it is how people understand the world around them and identify appropriate ways of conducting themselves in the many different environments they may occupy (Delle)

Now with an understanding of this above mentioned fact, we know that all a man does are social activities; each and every social activity requires space for movement and specific amount of energy whether mental or physical; each and every social activity need a certain amount of time to be completed as well as frequency of occurrence. If we could have, instead of land management, observed these social movement pattern of human beings based on their intent, desires, needs and motivation and then spatially imprint such activities and then analyze their types; required social energy and actual energy spent; frequency of their occurrence; and interference of each other, sub-imposing or super-imposing then we may classify such activities based on their types and level of social energy required; create Hubs for such classified activities and place them in such a manner that they do not interfere into the path of movement of each other and their spatial distance from the man is based on their types and social activity energy level then we will come up with an urban settlement plan which is based on socio-cultural aspects of human beings and their behavior. I would like to call it Socio-Cultural Harmonic Urban Planning

Hence the remedies to almost all the socio-cultural problems, human beings are facing in urban dwellings, are only in the socio-cultural approach in the establishment of human urban settlements based on these very basic and integral building blocks of a society as mentioned above and return the much lost happiness to the inhabitants. Furthermore, man has this characteristic, embedded in genetic code, of feeling happiness, joy and pleasure in the company of his nuclear family, extended family and friends and such relations build over a long period of time with the investment of many years, within a specific social boundary. Any weakening of this core effects the livelihood and level of happiness and joy and all provisions must be provided to maximize or optimize strengthening of such traits and conditions of social and cultural aspects of human living. Spatially, this could be achieved by developing Family Cells and Neighborhoods or Mohallas (subdivisions) logically and by providing all the related social facilities and activity centers associated with a society from lower to higher social activity energy levels or (and) social activity types and at approximately equal distances or (and) harmonically to all these residential Family Cells and Neighborhoods or Muhallas of the related societies such that social activity hubs with lower social activity energy or types built around their corresponding higher social activity energy hubs and vice versa

This is important in order to bring discipline, equality, harmony and standardization in human settlement and urbanization and minimize development and mobilization costs, so that inhabitants may have more time to sit together and nourish the spiritual being of each other, develop relations, friendships and communities. This can only be effective if men evolve long lasting relationship with land, relatives and family and minimize migration from one place to another in search of better material living. This can be possible if urban landscape is based on socio-cultural aspects of human living. This is how human societies and urban settlements should be developed instead of what we have now--huge clusters of concretes, materials and metals spreading over an area haphazardly and in a disorganized manner without harmony and logical connections among the constituting socio-cultural components of a human urban settlement

Hence, again as mentioned above, according to the underlying principles, in the proposed method of human settlements and urbanizations, not only the social activity areas related to human societies are concentrated into hubs classified based on social activity energy levels or (and) types but these hubs are spatially placed in a uniformly and harmonically distributed manner, with hubs related to the lower most social activity energy levels or (and) logically related unique types encircling or surrounding the corresponding hub related to higher social activity energy levels or (and) logically related unique types at approximately equal intervals of space, which in turn is encircling the next higher level hub with further higher level of social activity energy levels or (and) logically related unique social activity types and vice versa, with residential units surrounding the hubs with lowest social activity energy levels or (and) logically related unique social activity types only, in such a way that the movement of human beings may be optimal and without any interference with other aspects and activities of the society

Furthermore, if you look closely at the standard layout, you would find out the urban development is not haphazard but transitioning uniformly and harmonically from lower most social activity energy levels or (and) logically related unique social activity types to the comparatively higher most social activity energy levels or (and) logically related unique social activity types and vice versa. This phenomenon is then occurring and re-occurring at equal intervals in the space

SPATIAL REPRESENTATION:

The drawings referred to herein provide examples of applications of the above mentioned method of development of human urban settlement areas and infrastructure and may not necessarily be referred to as the exact or (and) complete representation of Socio-Cultural Harmonic Urban Planning. This method of human settlement may have numerous forms of manifestations as per ideas envisaged within this urban planning. A Diagram has been presented here to understand basic idea regarding how to evolve the idea of Socio-Cultural Harmonic Urban Human Settlement and urbanization as follows:

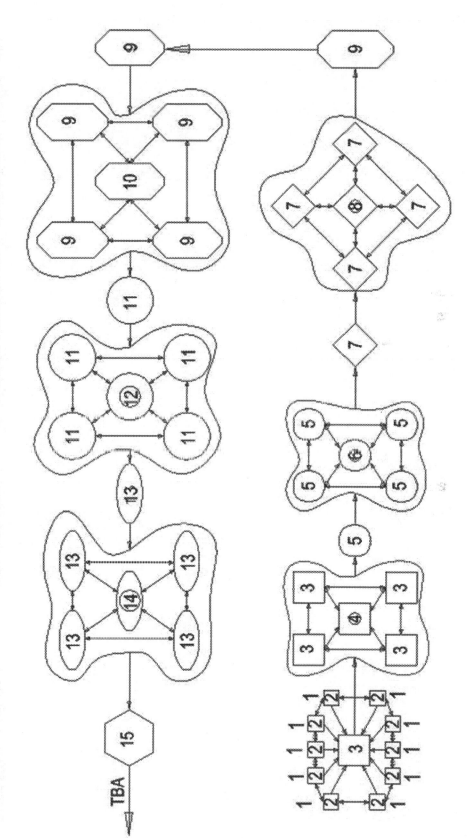

FAMILY CELL= 1
NEIGHBORHOOD STRATUM= 5
SOCIAL STRATUM= 9
NATIONAL STRATUM= 13

PRIVATE HUB= 2
COMMUNITY HUB= 6
INDUSTRIAL HUB= 10
UNIVERSAL HUB= 14

PRIVATE STRATUM= 3
COMMUNITY STRATUM= 7
INDUSTRIAL STRATUM= 11
UNIVERSAL STRATUM= 15

NEIGHBORHOOD HUB= 4
SOCIAL HUB= 8
NATIONAL HUB= 12
HIGHER LEVEL IF ANY= TBA

TBA

In order to further explain the phenomenon, the following elements have been designated numbers as follows:

Family Cell= 1; Private Hub= 2; Private Stratum or Domain= 3; Neighborhood Hub= 4; Neighborhood Stratum or Domain= 5; Community Hub= 6; Community Stratum or Domain= 7, Social Hub= 8; Social Stratum or Domain= 9; Industrial Hub= 10; Industrial Stratum or Domain = 11; National Hub= 12; National Stratum or Domain= 13; Universal Hub= 14; Universal Stratum or Domain= 15; Privways= 16; Neighborways= 17; Commways= 18; Socioways= 19; Indusways= 20; Nationways= 21; Uniways= 22; Sociorails= 23; Indusrails= 24; Nationrails= 25; Unirails= 26; Sociolines= 27; Induslines= 28; Nationlines= 29; Unilines= 30; Interchange= 31

In order to understand this idea of Socio-Cultural Harmonic Human Settlements and Urbanization in a better way or manner, I have represented this idea in the form of drawings with the help of examples as follows:

FIG. 1 shows or illustrates example of a Universal Stratum or Domain and rel. hub

FIG. 2 shows or illustrates example of a National Stratum or Domain and rel. hub

FIG. 3 shows or illustrates example of an Industrial Stratum or Domain and rel. hub

FIG. 4 shows or illustrates example of a Social Stratum or Domain and rel. hub

FIG. 5 shows or illustrates example of a Community Stratum or Domain and rel. hub

FIG. 6 illustrates example of a Neighborhood Stratum or Domain and rel. hub

FIG. 7 shows or illustrates example of a Private Stratum or Domain and rel. hub

FIGs. 8A and 8B show or illustrate examples of Community Transport Systems

FIGs. 9A and 9B illustrate examples of Industrial Mass Transit Systems

FIGs. 10A and 10B illustrate show examples of National Transit Systems

FIGs. 11A and 11B show examples of National Mass Transit Systems

FIG. 12 shows or illustrates Procedure Chart showing the evolution of a Socio-Cultural Harmonic Urban Planning and Human Settlement

Now coming back to the explanation regarding the proposed human settlement and urbanization as follows:

All the human related social activity centers are concentrated in hubs classified from lower social activity energy levels or (and) logically related unique social activity types to higher social activity energy levels or (and) logically related unique social activity types. A logical classification may be called Private Hubs **2**, Neighborhood Hubs **4**, Community Hubs **6**, Social Hubs **8,** Industrial Hubs **10**, National Hubs **12** and Universal Hubs **14**. Examples are as shown in the drawings

Family Cells **1s** are created by building residential units around the hub with lower most social activity energy levels or (and) types of social activities uniquely related to private or (and) family living only and is called Private Hub **2**, for example, as shown in the FIG 7

A Private Stratum or Domain **3** is created by developing and linking these Family Cells **1s** with each other, for example, as shown in the FIG 7

A Neighborhood Stratum or Domain **5** is then created by making the corresponding Private Strata or Domains **3s** to be built around a Neighborhood Hub **4** at approximately equal intervals in space, for example as shown in FIG 6

A Community Stratum or Domain **7** is then created by making the corresponding Neighborhood Strata or Domains **5s** to be built around a Community Hub **6** at approximately equal intervals of space, for example, as shown in the FIG 5

A Social Stratum or Domain **9** is then created by making the corresponding Community Strata or Domains to be built around a Social Hub **8** at approximately equal intervals of space, for example, as shown in the FIG 4

An Industrial Stratum or Domains **11** is then created by making the corresponding Social Strata or Domains **9s** to be built around an Industrial Hub **10** at approximately equal intervals of space, for example, as shown in the FIG 3

A National Stratum or Domain **13** is then created by making corresponding Industrial Strata or Domains **11s** to be built around a National Hub **12** at approximately equal intervals of space, for example, as shown in the FIG 2

A Universal Stratum or Domain **15** is then created by making corresponding National Strata or Domains **13s** to be built around Universal Hub **14** at approximately equal intervals of space, for example, as shown in the FIG 1

Developing a spatially uniform and harmonic pattern of above mentioned human settlements and urbanizations on earth; and more Strata may be added or (and) inserted within the above mentioned strata as per the requirements as well as 2 or more Strata may be merged together to form single Stratum

Human beings are social animals and may not survive feasibly and optimally without the help and support of fellow beings. A society allows its members to achieve needs or wishes they could not fulfill alone; there are social facts that can be identified, understood or specified within a circumstance that certain resources, objectives, requirements or results, are needed and utilized in an individual manner and for individual ends, although they can't be achieved, gotten or fulfilled in an individual manner as well, but, on the contrary, they can be gotten only in a collective, collaborative manner. Therefore, human beings formed societies under the common sense of individual interests

A society is a place where human beings live, communicate, share and work with each other towards the achievements of their individual goals and interests. Thus man need places to socialize but at the same time need moments of solitude and family privacy as well to enjoy the fruits of his achievements. The proposed method of human settlement and urban development is based upon the transition of these very basic human characteristics in an organized, uniformed and harmonic manner. The proposed principle aspects have been computed and designed in such a way that not even single aspect allows unnecessary interaction among people of different communities, areas and domain of social activities

Family Cell is the most important component or element of the proposed human settlement and urbanization. It should be a closed boundary development with suitable number of houses with their backyard connected so that the residents and dwellers may come together physically in direct communication with each other and build long lasting friendships and social relations. The occupants should preferably be relations or close friends or they intend to build close friendships and social relations. The provision of jogging tracks, play areas for children, meeting places for adults and children etc provide places of solitude and private family life within the social boundaries of Nuclear Families, Extended Families and friends. Meetup places, parks, play grounds, lakes, notice boards, libraries, elementary schools etc. would provide opportunity for families to regularly meet and develop and strengthen neighborhood. Neighborhoods are the spatial entities with which the corresponding residents evolve a long lasting or lifelong affiliations which transfer from generations to generation and necessary for the success of a social setup and achievement of individual goals related to the social contract and associated happiness; The provision of secondary or high schools, community centers, gymnasiums, health and exercise clubs or centers, indoor sports complexes, computer labs, community level social activity centers, clinics, municipal offices and administrative wards, etc., act as a domain for communities; Colleges, technical and higher learning institutes, technical and non-technical higher learning institutes, malls, plazas, shopping centers, IT centers, corporate offices, banks and other financial and commercial institutes, hospitals, transportation hubs, recreational centers, social clubs, cinemas, etc., are places where people comprising of various backgrounds and from miscellaneous communities, nationalities and background may meet on social scale and help develop a well disciplined, balanced and uniform society; Then there comes provision of high volume commodity production facilities, industries, high tech universities, manufacturing facilities, fabrication facilities, workshops, assembly plants, all types of production units, non-hazardous processing plants, information technology centers and other facilities which come within high energy social activities; Then there comes provision of all social activity platforms related to social energy on national levels such as national or (and) State controlled universities and educational centers of national repute and importance, provincial and national legislative assemblies, high courts, national bureaucratic and administrative offices, arts councils, cultural centers, gymnasiums, national museums, warehouses, high speed mass transportation or transit system, intercity railway stations, heavy industries, intercity bus terminals, dry ports, hotels, national parks and other related necessary facilities to sustain this hub and which come within the definition of a national setup; These social setups are uniformly connected through Universal Stratum or Links to access and connect to other societies of the world via airport and other very high speed transportation systems, embassies and consulates, supreme courts, museums, international bureaucratic and administrative offices, research centers, heavy industries of international importance, universities and educational centers of international repute and importance, 5 star and above hotels, resorts, water parks, forests preserves, recreational centers, stadiums, camping areas etc. and other related necessary facilities to sustain this hub and which come within definition of a universal or global setup. Agricultural lands and irrigation systems should be a part of such setup. We may also put agricultural activities as the next higher type social activity and create a separate hub for such activities called Agrarian Hub and then develop Universal Strata around this Agrarian Hub

Hence this way the whole Urban Area may be classified into less or more 7 or 8 basic Strata according to the social energy levels as follows: Family Cell or Domain **1s**, Private Stratum or Domain **3**, Neighborhood Stratum or Domain **5**,

Community Stratum or Domain **7**, Social Stratum or Domain **9**, Industrial Stratum or Domain **11**, National Stratum or Domain **13** and then, Universal Stratum or Domain **15** and then may be Agrarian Stratum

FAMILY CELLS AND PRIVATE STRATUM OR DOMAIN:

The building cell or block of this proposed method of development of human settlement urban areas and infrastructure, as shown in FIG 7, is Family Cell **1** which is formed when residential structures are built around a Private Hub **2** with lowest social activity levels or (and) logically related types. These Family Cells **1s** are developed and linked with each other harmonically and uniformly in space to form a Private Stratum or Domain **3** which are then built at approximately equal intervals of space around the corresponding next higher level human social activity hub based on social activity types or (and) energy levels hence forming next higher level of Stratum or Domain which in turn, though may not exactly, are built at approximately equal intervals of space around the corresponding further higher level hub based on social activity types or (and) energy levels and vice versa thus creating a harmonic pattern of hubs and strata with lower to higher to lower social activity types or (and) energy levels and vice versa

As per the method of developing the proposed type of human settlement urbanization as described in FIG 7, a Private Stratum or Domain **3** is built such that families preferably alongwith relatives and friends may live in complete privacy, building relations and friendships without any trespassing while sharing only those aspects of a society which may not disturb their private living as social beings and participants of the proposed social setup. This is the place where individuals enjoy the fruits of their earnings and successes with related families, relations and friends. A Private Hub **2** may be of any size and shape as per the geographical and cultural aspects and requirements from place to place and nation to nation and should not have any provision for business, trading, politics or financial activities and facilities etc. but has provision for social activities logically related to a Private or (and) Family setup with social activity types unique and different than the social activities in other Hubs or (and) social activity energy levels lower than the consecutive higher social activity energy level Hubs. The Private Hub **2**, though not necessarily exactly, but is built approximately at the center of Family houses **1s** to maintain the true harmonic character of proposed stratum

A Family Cell **1** may be of any suitable size and shape but preferably 200m*100m in area. The residents of a Family Cell **1** within their premises do have all the facilities which come within the definition of Private living setup hence providing places of social interaction supporting the family life such as play areas for the children, adults and elders, party places, physical exercise areas, meetup place to spend quality time etc. The residents of Family Cells **1s** may share and have access to the Private Hub **2** to avail the related facilities preferably through their rear doors in their common backyard. The idea is to provide the residents a place where children may play in complete safety of their privately secured common backyard where no one from outside world may enter or interrupt their private family living. Where adults and youngsters may warm up, do physical exercises and jog around to keep themselves fit, sit together around a park table, chat, laugh and communicate. Where household ladies meet and discuss their issues etc. A place where this all could be done without compromising their privacy and safety is the essence of Family Cells **1s** and Private Stratum or Domain **3**

The whole stratum may be surrounded by footpaths, amenities aisles, streets and green belts of suitable width with trees of considerable heights and all types of provisions as per contemporary requirements and standards. The houses within this stratum or domain should be comprised of basement, ground floor, 1ˢᵗ floor and 2ⁿᵈ floor or upto 4 levels to achieve an optimal density

An example of Private Stratum or Domain **3** is shown in FIG 7. A Private Stratum or Domain as shown is one of the many sizes and shapes it may take. In this example, many residential houses around a Private Hub **2** are forming a Family Cell **1** which in turn are arranged in space uniformly or (and) harmonically to create a Private Stratum or Domain **3**. This Family Cell **1** is the Building Block of the proposed urban planning. The Privways **16** or Harmonic Roadways System HRS Level-1 are built around these Family Cells **1s** as shown in FIG 7, connecting the Private Strata **3s** to Neighborhood Hub **4** through the intersection of Privways **16** or HRS Level-1 and Neighborways **17** or HRS Level-2. The Privways **16** or HRS Level-1 may have Exit-Entrance setup only along the periphery of Private Strata **3s** settlements. All the related social activity centers and platforms are located within the Private Hub **2**. There is only 1 restricted Exit and Entrance point for accessing the Private Hub **2**. As may be seen there are approximately 8 Family Cells **1s** built within an area of 500meters*500meters hence creating a Private Stratum or Domain **3**. The size and shape of Private Stratum or Domain **3** may vary from each other within their respective Neighborhood Stratum or Domain **5** as well

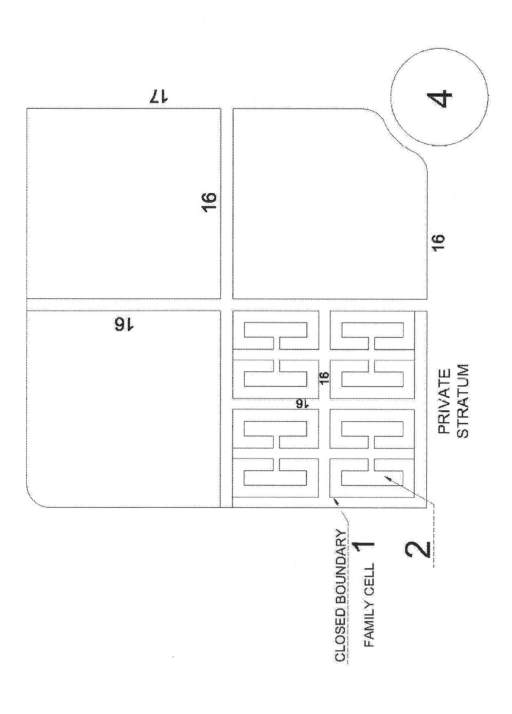

CLOSED BOUNDARY

FAMILY CELL 1

2

PRIVATE STRATUM

17

16

16

16

16

16

4

AN APPLICATION OF PRIVATE STRATUM 3 WITHIN THE PROPOSED
METHOD OF HUMAN SETTLEMENT AND URBANIZATION

FIG 7

NEIGHBORHOOD STRATUM OR DOMAIN:

A Neighborhood Stratum or Domain **5** is formed when 2 or more but preferably 4 Private Strata or Domains **3s** are uniformly and harmonically built around a Neighborhood Hub **4**. This is a place where residents of Private Strata or Domains **3s** come together, live a life as neighbors, performing relatively higher energy level social activities or (and) logically related unique social activities, building relations and friendships as neighbors within a boundary without trespassing. A Neighborhood Hub **4** though not necessarily exactly, but is built approximately and reasonably at the center of Neighborhood Stratum or Domain **5**. This Hub may be of any size and shape as per the geographical and national requirements and may be carved out of the Private Strata or Domains **3s** surrounding this hub. A Neighborhood Hub **4** has no provision for business, trading, politics or financial activities and facilities etc but has provision for social activities logically related to a Neighborhood with types unique and different than the social activities in other Hubs or (and) energy level higher than the energy level of social activities in Private Hubs **2s** but lower than the consecutive higher social activity energy level Hubs. A Neighborhood Hub **4** may have less or more of following facilities: Primary or elementary learning schools, play grounds, library, fitness centers, notice boards, meeting places, parks and other activities and facilities which come within the definition of Neighborhood level activities

A Neighborhood Stratum or Domain **5** though may not exactly, with the same or variable sizes and shapes, but is built at approximately equal intervals of space within a Community Stratum **7** or (and) around Community Hub **6**. The size and shape of this Stratum is governed by the numbers, sizes and shapes of the Private Stratum **3** within this stratum but preferably should be within an area of 1Km*1Km. The whole stratum is surrounded by footpaths, amenities aisles, roads and forest belts of suitable width with trees of considerable heights. There are provided, though not necessarily, preferably only two entrance and exit points to the Neighborhood Stratum or Domain **5**, so that the movements of all types may well be monitored and controlled as per requirements. The access to schools for pedestrians should be through underground corridors, thus providing, for children, safe and secured environment. This stratum or Domain design is proposed in such a manner that there cannot be any unintentional trespassing or there can only be intentional trespassing possible. With just 2 points for entering and exit and provision of steel fencing around the Neighborhood Stratum or Domain **5**, each and every entry may be monitored, recorded and controlled

An example of Neighborhood Stratum or Domain **5** is shown in FIG 6. A Neighborhood Stratum or Domain **5** as shown in the above mentioned drawing is one of the many shapes it may take. In this example, many Private Strata or Domains **3s** around a Neighborhood Hub **4** are forming a Neighborhood Stratum **5**. The Neighborways **17** or HRS Level-2 are emanating from the Neighborhood Hub **4** as shown and run along the periphery of Private Strata or Domains **3s** connecting the Private Strata or Domains **3s** to Neighborhood Hub **4** through the intersection of Privways **16** or HRS Level-1 and Neighborways **17** or HRS Level-2. The Neighborways **17** or HRS Level-2 may have single Exit-Entrance setup only along the periphery of Private Strata or Domains **3s** settlements and then merge into the Commways **18** or HRS Level-3. All the related social activity centers and platforms are located within the Neighborhood Hub **4**. High rise residential buildings in Quarter-Circular-Belts may be built around Neighborhood Hub **4** to increase urban density as shown in the figures

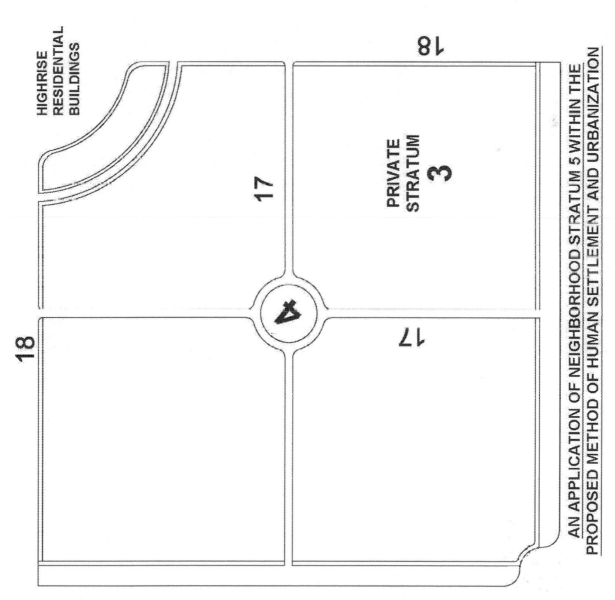

HIGHRISE RESIDENTIAL BUILDINGS

18

17

PRIVATE STRATUM
3

4

17

18

AN APPLICATION OF NEIGHBORHOOD STRATUM 5 WITHIN THE
PROPOSED METHOD OF HUMAN SETTLEMENT AND URBANIZATION

FIG 6

COMMUNITY STRATUM OR DOMAIN:

A Community Stratum or Domain **7** is formed when 2 or more but preferably 4 Neighborhood Strata or Domains **5s** are built around a Community Hub **6**, which is the place where the residents of Neighborhood Strata **5** come together and communicate with each other in order to form a community and get a common platform for the solution of their non-financial but community issues and administer related geographical area at community level

A Community Hub **6** though not necessarily exactly, but is located approximately and reasonably at the center of Community Stratum or Domain **7**. This Hub may be of any size and shape as per the geographical and cultural requirements and may be carved out of the Neighborhood Strata **5s** surrounding this hub. A Community Hub **6** has no provision for business, trading, politics or financial activities etc but has provision for social activities logically related to a community with types unique and different than the social activities in other hubs or (and) social activity energy levels higher than the energy levels of activities in Private Hubs **2s** and Neighborhood Hubs **4s** but lower than the consecutive higher level hubs. A Community Hub **6** may have less or more of the following facilities: High schools, community and technical colleges, indoor sports complex, municipality offices, police stations, community centers including marriage halls, computer and educational centers, spiritual centers, fitness and health centers and other facilities which come within the definition of a community level activities

A Community Stratum or Domain **7,** though may not exactly, with the same or variable sizes and shapes is built at approximately equal intervals of space within Social Stratum or Domain **9** or (and) around Social Hub **8**. The size of this Stratum or Domain is governed by the numbers, sizes and shapes of the Neighborhood Strata **5s** within this stratum or domain but preferably should be within an area of 2Kms*2Kms. The whole stratum or domain is preferably surrounded by footpaths, amenities aisles and forest belts of suitable width. This Hub is accessible by the residents through roads and underground corridors to connect the Neighborhood Strata **5s** with the Community Hub **6** for safe movement of pedestrians especially children. Again there are, though not necessarily, preferably total of only 2 entry and exit points for Community Stratum or Domain **7**. Thus the movements of all the entities can be monitored and controlled optimally

An example of Community Stratum or Domain **7** is shown in FIG 5. A Community Stratum or Domain **7** as shown in the above mentioned drawing is one of the many shapes it may take. In this example, 4 Neighborhood Strata **5s** together around a Community Hub **6** are forming a Community Stratum or Domain 7. The Commways **18** or HRS Level-3 are emanating from the Community Hub **6** as shown and run along the periphery of Neighborhood Strata **5s** connecting the Neighborhood Hubs **4s** to Community Hub **6** through the intersection of Neighborways **17** or HRS Level-2 and Commways **18** or HRS Level-3. The Commways **18** or HRS Level-3 may have single Exit-Entrance setup only along the periphery of each Neighborhood Stratum or Domain **5** and then may merge into the Socioways **19** or HRS Level-4. All the related social activity centers and platforms are located within the Community Hub **6**. There may be only 4 Exit and Entrance points for accessing the Community Hub

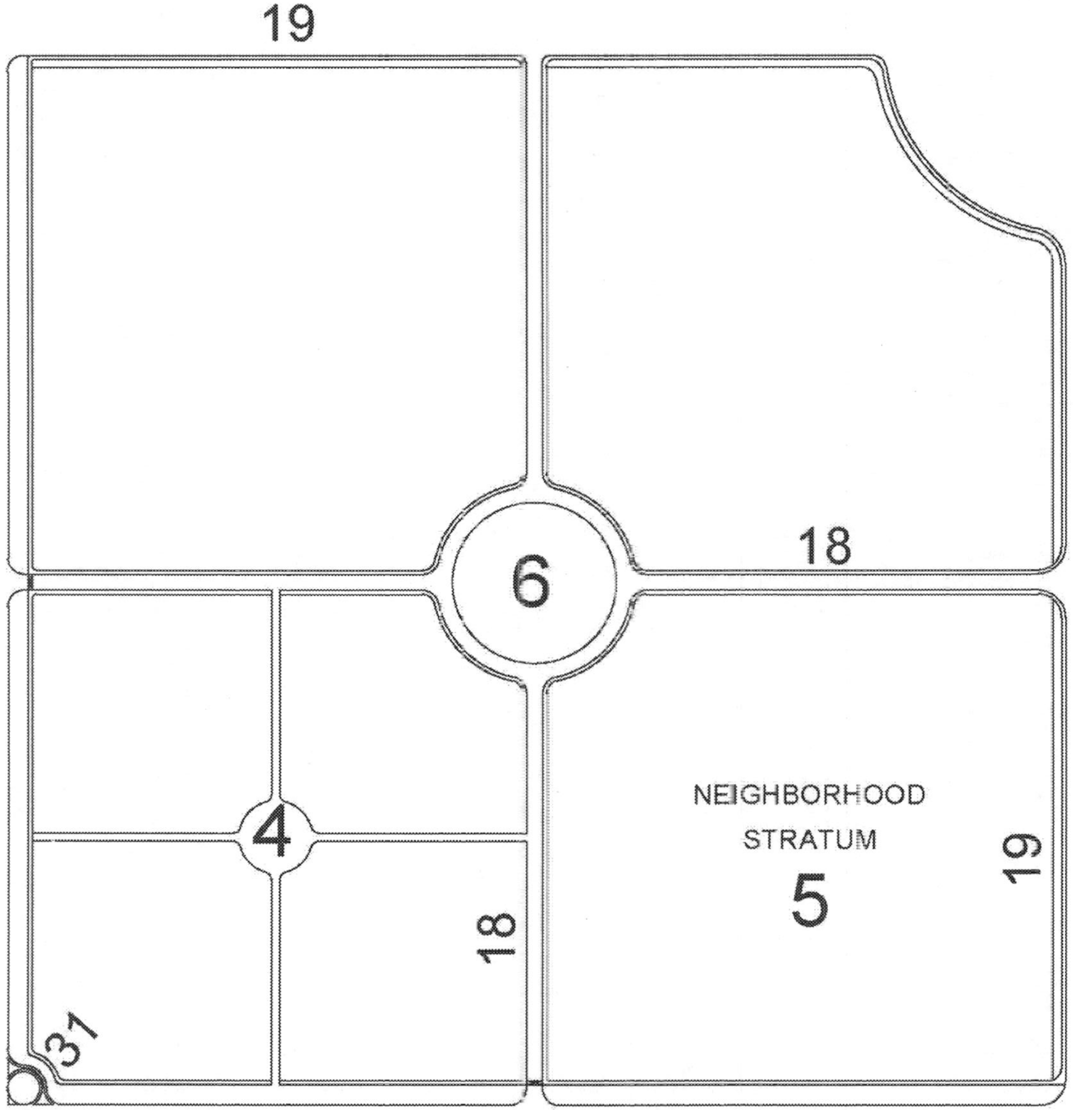

NEIGHBORHOOD STRATUM

5

19

18

18

6

19

4

37

AN APPLICATION OF COMMUNITY STRAT JM 7 WITHIN THE
PROPOSED MTHOD OF HUMAN SETTLEMENT AND URBANIZATION

FIG   5

SOCIAL STRATUM OR DOMAIN:

A Social Stratum or Domain **9** is formed when 2 or more but preferably 4 Community Strata or Domains **7s** are built around a Social Hub **8** which is the place to socialize, where residents from neighboring communities may come together, practice their social rights and responsibilities and perform activities as per logical definition of society and support each other individually and collectively, socially and economically and build a culture, hence establishing a Harmonic Society

The Social Hub **8**, though not necessarily, but is located approximately at the center of Social Stratum or Domain **8**. This Hub may be of any size and shape as per the geographical and cultural requirements and may be carved out of the Community Strata or Domains **7s** surrounding this hub. A Social Hub **8** has provision of business, trading, political, social and financial activities and other facilities and activities which come within the logical definition of Social activities with types unique and different than social activities in other Hubs or (and) energy levels higher than the energy levels of activities in Private Hubs **2s**, Neighborhood Hubs **4s** and Community Hubs **6s** but lower than the consecutive higher level Hubs. The Social Hub **8** has less or more of the following facilities: Malls, shopping centers, corporate offices, banks and other financial and commercial institutes, hospitals, gas stations and petrol pumps, showrooms, business outlets, service offices, restaurants, law offices, lower courts, recreational centers, helipads for flying cars, places for higher level socializations for cultural intermixing and harmony such as dance clubs, cinemas, theatres, art galleries council, recreational centers and other activities, technical institutes and degree awarding colleges and technical and universities and other facilities which come within the definition of higher level social activities

The Social Stratum or Domain **9** though may not exactly, with the same or variable sizes and shapes, but built at approximately equal intervals of space within the Industrial Stratum or Domain **11** or (and) around Industrial Hub **10**. The size of this Stratum or Domain is governed by the numbers, sizes and shapes of the Community Strata **7s** within this Stratum or domain but preferably should be within an area of 5Kms*5Kms. The whole Stratum or Domain is preferably surrounded by amenities aisles and footpaths of suitable width. The Community Strata **7s** are connected to the Social Hub **8** through roadways and underground corridors. There should be four exit and entry points available to access the Social Stratum or Domain **9**. Thus the movements of all the entities can be checked and controlled

An example of Social Stratum or Domain is shown in FIG 4. A Social Stratum or Domain as shown is one of the many shapes it may take. In this example, 4 Community Strata or Domains 7s together around a Social Hub 8 are forming a Social Stratum or Domain **9**. The Socioways **19** or HRS Level-4 are emanating from the Social Hub **8** as shown and run along the periphery of Community Strata **7s** connecting the Community Hubs **6s** to Social Hub **8** through the interchanges at the intersection of Commways **18** or HRS Level-3 and Socioways **19** or HRS Level-4. The Socioways **19** may have single Exit-Entrance setup only along the periphery of each Community Stratum or Domain 7 as well as interchanges at intersections of Socioways **19**-Socioways **19** or HRS Level-4--Level-4, Socioways **19**-Indusways **20** or HRS Level-4--Level-5, Socioways **19**-Nationways **21** or HRS Level-4--Level-6 and Socioways **19**-Uniways **22** or HRS Level-4--Level-7 only depending upon the location and orientation orientation of the Social Stratum or Domain. All the related social activity centers and platforms are located within the Social Hub **8**

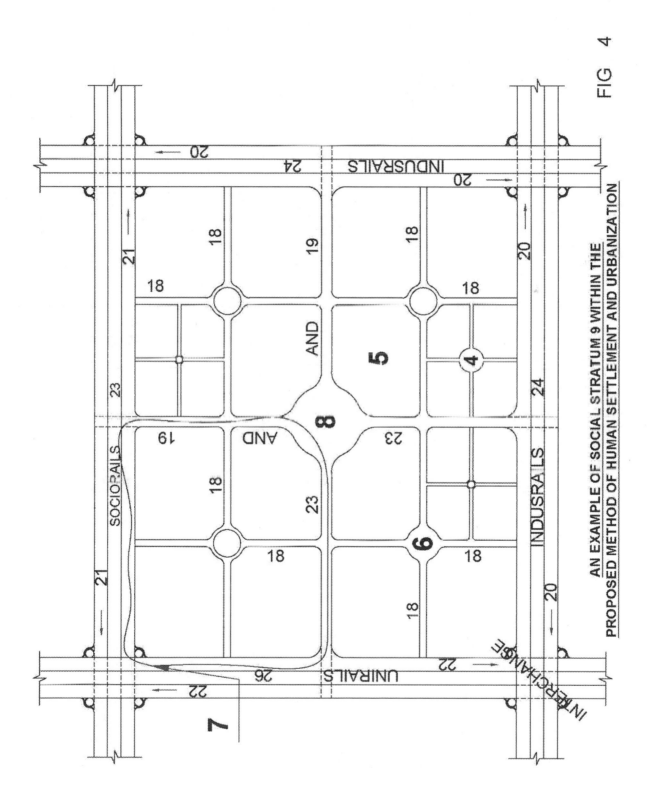

AN EXAMPLE OF SOCIAL STRATUM 9 WITHIN THE
PROPOSED METHOD OF HUMAN SETTLEMENT AND URBANIZATION

FIG 4

INDUSTRIAL STRATUM OR DOMAIN:

An Industrial Stratum or Domain **11** is formed when 2 or more but preferably 4-8 Social Strata or Domains **9s** are built around an Industrial Hub **10** which is the place where the residents of Social Strata or Domains **9s** may come together and support each other towards the achievement of their individual goals and interests and work collectively for the sustainability of corresponding society by production of commodities and products on large scale with a sense of unified urban or civic identity and interests. Industrial society refers to a mass society driven by the use of technology to enable mass production, supporting a large population with a high capacity for division of labor. Industrial Hub **10** would be characterized by a society integrated with information technology as well

The Industrial Hub **10**, though not necessarily, but is located approximately at the center of Industrial Stratum or Domain **11**. An Industrial Hub **10** may be of any size and shape as per the geographical and cultural requirements and may be carved out of the Social Strata or Domains **9s** surrounding this hub. An Industrial Hub **10** has provision of social activities with types unique and different than the social activities in other Hubs or (and) social activity energy levels higher than Private Hubs **2s**, Neighborhood Hubs **4s**, Community Hubs **6s** and Social Hubs **8s** but lower than the consecutive higher level Hubs such as mass scale production of commodities characterized by the use of science and technologics including information technologies to sustain this hub and which come within logical definition of an Industrial Setup. Industrial Hub **10** has less or more of the following facilities:

Industries, manufacturing facilities, fabrication facilities, workshops, assembly plants, all types of production units, printing presses, non-hazardous processing plants, helipads for flying cars, power supply generations and related stations, amenities supply stations, privately owned higher educational and training centers and universities (offering degrees upto Masters level), information technology centers and other facilities which come within the definition of high energy social activities

The Industrial Stratum or Domain **11**, though may not exactly, with same or variable sizes and shapes is built at approximately equal intervals of space within National Stratum or Domain **13** or (and) around National Hub **12**. The size of this Stratum or Domain is governed by numbers, sizes and shapes of Social Strata or Domains **9s** within this Stratum or domain but preferably should be within an area of 10Kms*Kms or 15Kms*15Kms. The whole Stratum or Domain is preferably surrounded by amenities aisles of suitable width. The Social Strata or Domains **9s** are connected to the Industrial Hub **10** through roadways, railways and flyways

An example of Industrial Stratum or Domain **11** is shown in FIG 3. An Industrial Stratum or Domain **11** as shown is one of the many shapes it may take. In this example, 8 Social Strata or Domains **8s** together around an Industrial Hub **10** are forming an Industrial Stratum or Domain **11**. The Indusways **20** or HRS Level-5 are running at the periphery of Social Strata or Domains **9s** connecting Social Hubs **8s** to Industrial Hub **10** through interchanges at the intersection of Socioways **19** or HRS Level-4 and Indusways **20** or HRS Level-5. The Indusways **20** or HRS Level-5 may have many Exit-Entrance ramps only along the periphery of Industrial Hub **10** as well as interchanges at the intersections of Socioways **19**-Indusways **20** or HRS Level-4--Level-5, Indusways **20**-Indusways **20** or HRS Level-5--Level-5, Indusways **20**-Nationways **21** or HRS Level-5--Level-6 and Indusways **20**-Uniways **22** or HRS Level-5--Level-7 only

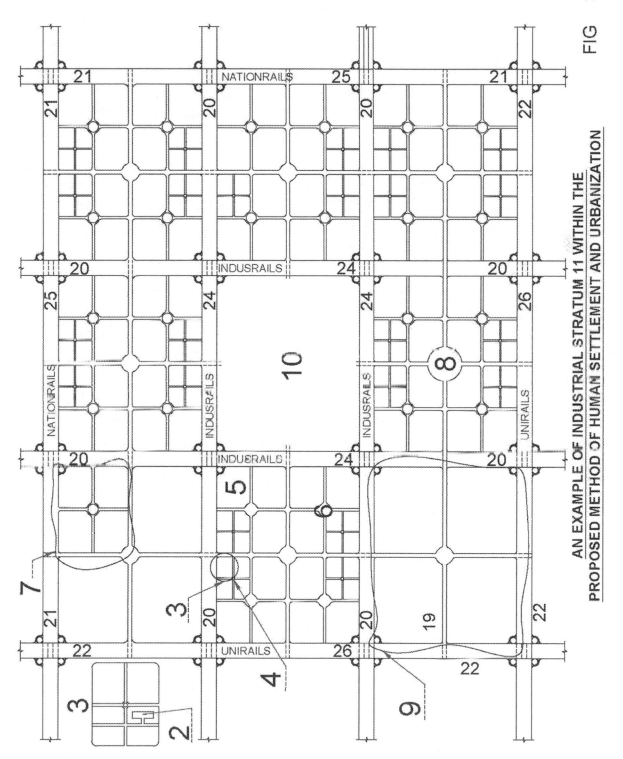

AN EXAMPLE OF INDUSTRIAL STRATUM 11 WITHIN THE
PROPOSED METHOD OF HUMAN SETTLEMENT AND URBANIZATION

FIG 3

NATIONAL STRATUM OR DOMAIN:

A National Stratum or Domain **13** is formed when 2 or more but preferably 4 to 8 Industrial Strata or Domains **11** are built around a National Hub **12**, which is the place where the residents of Social Strata or Domains **9s** connect with other societies on national levels or (and) as citizens. This is a place where the residents may support each other collectively towards the achievement of their national and State interests and benefits in all aspects. A National Stratum or Domain **13,** though may not exactly, with the same or variable sizes and shapes is built at approximately equal intervals of space within Universal Stratum or Domain **15** or (and) around Universal Hub **14.** A National Hub **12** may be of any size and shape as per the geographical and cultural requirements and may be carved out of the Industrial Strata or Domains **11** surrounding this hub. The National Hub **12** though not necessarily or exactly, but is located approximately at the center of National Stratum or Domain **13** and almost all the related facilities are provided within this Hub in order to facilitate in maintaining the true harmonic characteristics of the proposed Stratum or Domain. A National Hub **12** has provision of social activities with types unique and different than the social activities in other Hubs or (and) social activity energy levels higher than Private Hubs **2s,** Neighborhood Hubs **4s,** Community Hubs **6s,** Social Hubs **8s,** and Industrial Hubs **10s,** but lower than the Universal Hubs **14s** as well as consecutive higher level Hubs, if any, such as all types of activities logically related to national and State affairs and other related necessary facilities to sustain this hub and which come within the definition of a National Setup

A National Hub **12** has less or more of the following facilities: Provincial or National legislative assemblies, high courts, national bureaucratic and administrative offices, warehouses, army garrison, helipads for helicopters and flying cars, railways stations, intercity bus terminals, dry ports, National or State controlled universities and educational centers of national repute and importance, arts councils, cultural centers, hotels and other related necessary facilities to sustain this hub. The size of this Stratum or Domain is governed by the numbers, sizes and shapes of the Industrial Strata **11s** within this Stratum or domain but preferably should be within an area of 20-30Kms*20-30Kms. The whole Stratum or Domain is preferably surrounded by amenities aisles of suitable width. The Industrial Strata or Domains **11s** are connected to National Hub **12** through roadways, railways and flyways. There should be many exit and entry points available to access the National Hub **12**

An example of National Stratum or Domain **13** is shown in FIG 2. A National Stratum or Domain **13** is one of the many shapes it may take. In this example, 4 Industrial Strata or Domains **11s** together around a National Hub **12** are forming a National Stratum or Domain **13.** The Nationways **21** or HRS Level-6 are running at the periphery of Industrial Strata or Domains **11s** connecting the Industrial Hubs **10s** to National Hub **12** through the interchanges at the intersection of Indusways **20** or HRS Level-5 and Nationways **21** or HRS Level-6. The Nationways **21** or HRS Level-6 may have many Exit-Entrance ramps only along the periphery of National Hub **12** as well as interchanges at the intersections of Socialways **19**-Nationways **21** or HRS Level-4--Level-6, Indusways **20**-Nationways **21** or HRS Level-5--Level-6, Nationways **21**-Nationways **21** or HRS Level-6--Level-6 and Nationways **21**-Uniways **22** or the HRS Level-6--Level-7 only. All the related social activity centers and platforms are located within the National Hub **12**

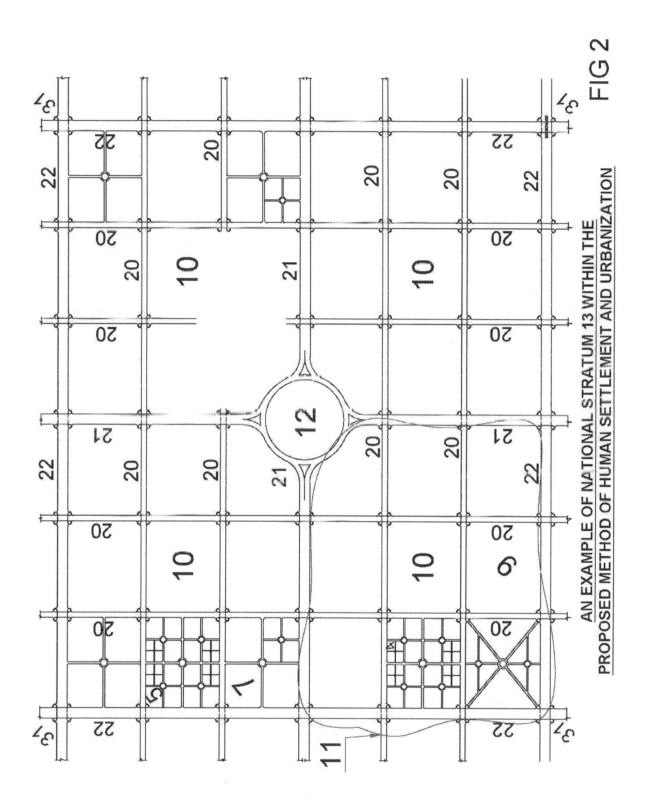

AN EXAMPLE OF NATIONAL STRATUM 13 WITHIN THE
PROPOSED METHOD OF HUMAN SETTLEMENT AND URBANIZATION

FIG 2

UNIVERSAL OR GLOBAL STRATUM OR DOMAIN:

A Universal Stratum or Domain **15** is formed when 2 or more but preferably 4-8 National Strata or Domains **13s** are built around Universal Hub **14**, which is the place where the residents of a society connect with their fellows from other societies on universal and global levels. This is a place where the residents may support each other collectively towards the achievement of their goals as human race with all related interests, activities and benefits in all aspects. Agriculture and irrigation system should be an integral part of this Stratum or Domain and enough land should be available in Universal Hub **14** to produce agricultural products to sustain the related society. The Universal Hub **14**, though not necessarily and exactly is located approximately at the center of Universal Stratum or Domain **15** and almost all the related facilities are provided within this Hub

A Universal Hub **15** may be of any size and shape as per the geographical and cultural requirements and may be carved out of the National Strata **13s** surrounding this hub. Universal Hub **14** has provision of social activities with types unique and different than the social activities in other Hubs or (and) social activity energy levels higher than the Private Hubs **2s**, Neighborhood Hubs **4s**, Community Hubs **6s**, Social Hubs **8s**, Industrial Hubs **10s** and National Hubs **12s** but lower than the consecutive higher level Hubs if any, such as all types of activities logically related to universal affairs as well as agricultural and other related necessary facilities to sustain this Hub and which come within the definition of a Universal Setup. The Universal Hub **14** has less or more of the following facilities:

Agricultural lands, fruit orchards, fisheries, airports, water parks, international level recreational centers, embassies and consulates, forest preserves, camping areas, supreme courts, international bureaucratic and administrative offices, universities and educational centers of international repute and importance, helipads for helicopters and flying cars, hotels, golf clubs and other related necessary facilities to sustain this hub and which come within the definition of a Universal Setup. The size of this Stratum or Domain is governed by the numbers, sizes and shapes of National Strata or Domains **13s** within this Stratum or Domain but preferably should be within an area of 60-90Kms*60-90Kms

The whole Stratum or Domain is preferably surrounded by amenities aisles of suitable width. The National Strata or Domains **13s** are connected to Universal Hub **14** through roadways, railways and flyways. There should be many exit and entry points available to access the Universal Hub **14**. Regarding Airports, I would suggest more than 1 airport in the Universal Stratum or Domain

An example of Universal Stratum or Domain **15** is shown in FIG 1. A Universal Stratum or Domain **15** is one of the many shapes it may take. In this example, 8 National Strata or Domains **13s** together around a Universal Hub **14** are forming a Universal Stratum or Domain **15**. The Uniways **22** or HRS Level-7 are running at the periphery of National Strata or Domains **13s** connecting the National Hubs **12s** to Universal Hub **14** through the interchanges at the intersection of Nationways **21** or HRS Level-6 and Uniways **22** or HRS Level-7. An Interlink may run to connect the Nationways **21** or HRS Level-6 ending at the periphery of Universal Hub **14**. The Uniways **22** or HRS Level-7 may have many Exit-Entrance ramps only along periphery of Universal Hubs **14s** as well as the interchanges at intersections of Socioways **19**-Uniways **22** or HRS Level-4--Level-7, Indusways **20**-Uniways **22** HRS Level-5--Level-7, Nationways **21**-Uniways **22** or HRS Level-6--Level-7 and Uniways **22**-Uniways **22** or HRS Level-7--Level-7. All social activity centers and platforms are located within Universal Hub **14**

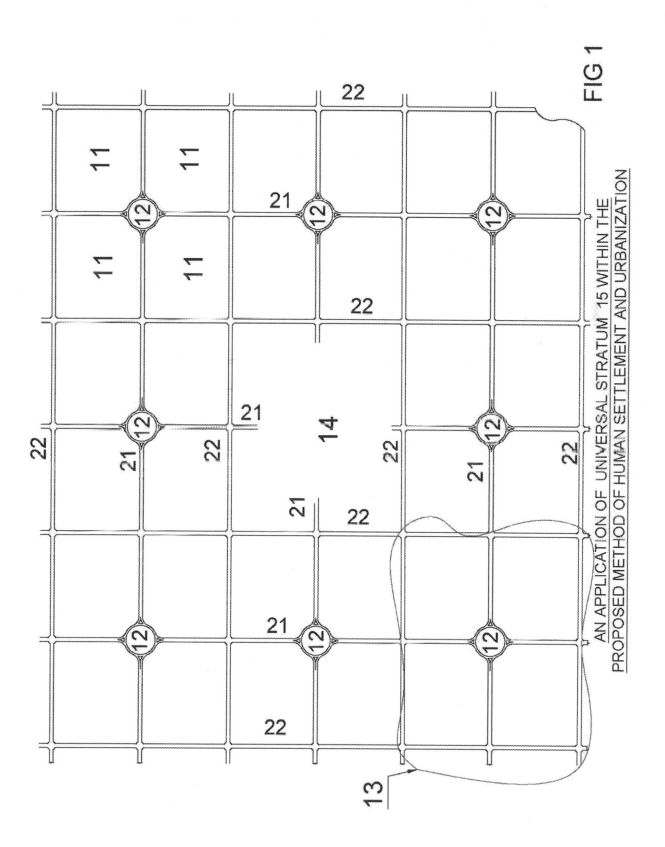

AN APPLICATION OF UNIVERSAL STRATUM 15 WITHIN THE
PROPOSED METHOD OF HUMAN SETTLEMENT AND URBANIZATION

FIG 1

Any two of the strata may be merged together or splitted as per the geographical and cultural requirements varying from nation to nation and country to country etc. The Universal Strata **15s** should be copied on land such that these Universal Strata **15s** are separated by water irrigation and supply belt 1km wide as shown in the Figures. Agricultural Stratum or Domain may be classified separately and there may be a higher Hub called Agrarian Hub with the Universal Strata encircling the Agrarian Hub. All related activities may then become a constituent of Agrarian Hub instead of the Universal Hubs such as agriculture, Farmlands, Orchards, greenlands etc

The above mentioned sequence may be considered reversed and instead of forming the Family Cells and Private Strata initially, we may form the Agrarian or Universal Stratum or Domain first and then build the corresponding lower level Stratum or Domain in the reverse sequence logically such as National Stratum or Domain around the Universal Hub and so on until we reach the Family Cells in the Private Stratum or Domain or the Private Domain. In such case the arrows in the Procedure or Flow Chart above may be reversed

SOCIO-CULTURAL HARMONIC TRANSPORTATION SYSTEMS

Regarding the method of development of Harmonic Roadways System, the social activity hubs of lowest social activity energy levels or (and) logically related unique types within their respective Stratum or Domain are connected to each other at the corresponding level through a specific road system. These hubs in a Stratum or Domain may not connect to the hubs of same types in another Stratum or Domain through the same specific road system. This whole setup would be considered as the Base-Level or Level 1 of the proposed Harmonic Roadways System. Such road system also connects the above mentioned lower level social activity energy levels or (and) types hubs to respectively higher level social activity energy level or (and) types hubs through a specifically higher level road system within their corresponding social Stratum or Domain at the intersecting interchanges

The next higher level road system may be called as Level 2 of the proposed Harmonic Roadways System. These Level 2 roadways connect the respective hubs with corresponding higher social activity energy levels or (and) types hubs within their respective Stratum or Domain as well as to the further higher social activity energy level or (and) types hubs within their respective Stratum or Domain through Level 3 of the proposed Harmonic Roadways System. This continues until this road system reaches the Universal Hubs **14s.** At Level-4 and higher these roadways system may connect to the same level roadways as well as higher level roadways within their respective Stratum or Domain as well as outside and adjacent same level Stratum or Domain.

HARMONIC ROADWAYS SYSTEM:

As an example of Harmonic Roadways System as shown in FIG 7, the Private Hubs **2s** are connected to each other through Level 1 of Harmonic Roadways System called Privways **16** within the same respective Neighborhood Stratum or Domain **5.** These Priveways **16** may not connect the respective Private Hubs **2s** of a Neighborhood Stratum or Domain **5** to the Private Hubs **2s** of other Neighborhood Strata **5s** within the next higher social activity energy levels or (and) types strata or domains called the Community Strata or Domains **7s.** These Privways **16** pour into the next higher level roadways system called Level 2 of the Harmonic Roadways System or Neighborways **17**, in order to connect these Private Hubs **2s** to their respective Neighborhood Hub **4** within the same Neighborhood Stratum or Domain **5.** These roadways may have tracks with any appropriate speed limit

As an example of Harmonic Roadways System as shown in FIG 6 and FIG 5, within a Community Stratum or Domain **7**, the respective Neighborhood Hubs **4s** are connected to each other through the Level-2 Neighborways **17.** These Neighborways **17** may not connect directly the respective Neighborhood Hubs **4s** of a Community Stratum or Domain **7** to Neighborhood Hubs **4s** of other Community Strata or Domains **7s** within the next higher social energy activity level Stratum or Domain called the Social Stratum or Domain **9.** These Neighborways **17s** connect to the next higher level roadways system called the Level 3 of the Harmonic Roadways System or Commways **18** in order to connect these Neighborhood Hubs to their respective Community Hub **6** within the same Community Stratum or Domain **7.** These roadways may have tracks with any appropriate speed limit

As an example of Harmonic Roadways System as shown in FIG 5 and FIG 4, within a Social Stratum or Domain **9** the respective Community Hubs **6s** are connected to each other through the Level 3 Commways **18.** These Commways **18** may not connect the respective Community Hubs **6s** of a Social Stratum or Domain **9** to Community Hubs **6s** of other Social Strata or Domains within the next higher social energy activity level Stratum or Domain called the Industrial Stratum or Domain **11.** These Commways **18** connect to the next higher level roadways system called the Socioways **19** in order to connect these Community Hubs **6s** to their respective Social Hub **8** within the same Social Stratum or Domain **9**, and may also or may not connect to the Indusways **20** and Nationways **21**. These Commways **18** may have tracks with any appropriate speed limit

As an example of Harmonic Roadways System as shown in FIG 4 and FIG 3, within an Industrial Stratum or Domain **11**, the respective Social Hubs **8s** are connected to each other through the Level-4 Socioways **19**. Socioways **19** may connect the Social Hubs **8s** of an Industrial Stratum or Domain **11** to each other and to the Social Hubs **8s** of other Industrial Strata **11s** within the next higher social energy activity level Stratum or Domain called the National Stratum or Domain **13**. These Socioways **19** pour into the next higher level roadways system called Indusways **20** in order to connect these Social Hubs **8s** to the Industrial Hub **10** of the same Industrial Stratum or Domain **11** and other Industrial Strata or Domains **11s** and may also connect to Nationways **21** as well as Uniways **22**. These Socioways **19** may have tracks of around 125 kmph or any suitable speed limits, connecting with hubs through Exit-Entrance ramps, and with the corresponding intersecting Socioways **19**, Indusways **20**, Nationways **21** and Uniways **22** through interchanges at Socioways **19**-Socioways **19**, Socioways **19**-Indusways **20**, Socioways **19**-Nationways **21** and Socioways **19**-Uniways **22** intersections. In addition to high speed land vehicles, all low level flying vehicles would also fly over the Socioways **19**

As an example of Harmonic Roadways System as shown in FIG 3 and FIG 2, within a National Stratum or Domain **13** respective Industrial Hubs **10s** are connected to each other through the Level-5 Indusways **20**. These Indusways **20** also connect the Industrial Hubs **10s** of a National Stratum or Domain **13** to each other and to Industrial Hubs **10s** of other National Strata or Domains **13s** within the next social energy activity level Stratum or Domain called the Universal Stratum or Domain **14**. These Indusways **20** connect to the next higher level roadways system called the Nationways **21** in order to connect these Industrial Hubs **10s** to National Hub **12** of same National Stratum or Domain **13** as well as other National Strata or Domains **13s** and also connect to Nationways **21** and Uniways **22**

These roadways may have tracks of appropriately high speed limits, connecting with hubs through Exit-Entrance ramps, and with the corresponding intersecting Socioways **19**, Indusways **20**, Nationways **21** and Uniways **22** through interchanges at Socioways **19**-Indusways **20**, Indusways **20**-Indusways **20**, Indusways **20**-Nationways **21** and Indusways **20**-Uniways **22** intersections. In addition to high speed land vehicles, all low level flying vehicles would also fly over these Indusways **20**

As an example of Harmonic Roadways System as shown in FIG 1 and FIG 2, within a Universal Stratum or Domain **15** the respective National Hubs **12** are connected to each other through the Level-6 Nationways **21**. These Nationways **21** may connect the National Hubs **12** of a Universal Stratum or Domain **15** to each other and to the National Hubs **12** of other Universal Strata or Domains **15s.** These Nationways **21** connect to the next higher level roadways system called the Uniways **22** in order to connect these National Hubs **12** to the Universal Hub **14** of same Universal Stratum or Domain **15.** These Uniways **22** connect all Universal Hubs **14s** to each other and may run theoretically indefinitely

These roadways may have tracks of around 200 Kms/hr or higher speed limits, connecting with hubs through Exit-Entrance ramps, and with the corresponding intersecting Socioways **19**, Indusways **20**, Nationways **21** and Uniways **22** through interchanges at Socioways **19**-Uniways **22**, Indusways **20**-Uniways **22**, Nationways **21**-Uniways **22** and Uniways **22**-Uniways **22** intersections. In addition to high speed land vehicles, all low level flying vehicles would also fly over Nationways **22** and Uniways **22**

HARMONIC MASS TRANSIT SYSTEM:

The Harmonic Mass Transit System is the transportation and mass mobilization system which operates between and among Social Activity Hubs and should not touch the outer fabrics of Neighborhoods and consists of Bus System and Railways System. The Harmonic Mass Transit System starts at lowest level from the Community Hubs **6s** and then continues to connect to respectively higher levels of Harmonic Mass Transit System until it reaches the Universal Hubs **14s.** In this system, within a Stratum or Domain, high speed buses or railcars connect the hubs of same social energy activity level or (and) the hubs of a specific social energy activity types and to hubs of corresponding next higher level of social energy activities without any intermediary stops or stations except within hubs and at intersections with same or higher level Mass Transit lines

Unirails **26** are developed connecting Universal Hubs **14s** with each other with intermittent stops only at the Intersecting Hubs and at intersection points with Nationrails **25**, Indusrails **24**, and Sociorails **23** in a series or parallel loop clockwise or (and) anticlockwise or (and) in a Back-Forth fashion between any 2 Universal Hubs **14s.** The speed limit should be higher than 250 Kmph. Railcar may make more than 1 stop within a hub. An example of Unirails is shown in FIG 11 A. This may also be given name based on their level as Level-4 Transit

Furthermore, high speed Nationrails **25** are developed connecting National Hubs **12s** with each other within their respective Universal Stratum or Domain **15** with the National Hubs **12s** of their immediate Universal Strata **15s** only; and with the Universal Hubs **14s** of their respective Universal Strata **15s** with intermittent stops only at the Hubs and at intersection points with Unirails **26**, Indusrails **24** and Sociorails **23** in a series or parallel loop clockwise or (and) anticlockwise or (and) in a Back-Forth fashion between 2 National Hubs **12s.** The speed limit should be around 250 Kmph. The railcar may make more than 1 stop within a hub. An example of the Nationrails is shown in FIG 11A and 11B. This may also be given name based on their level as Level-3 Transit

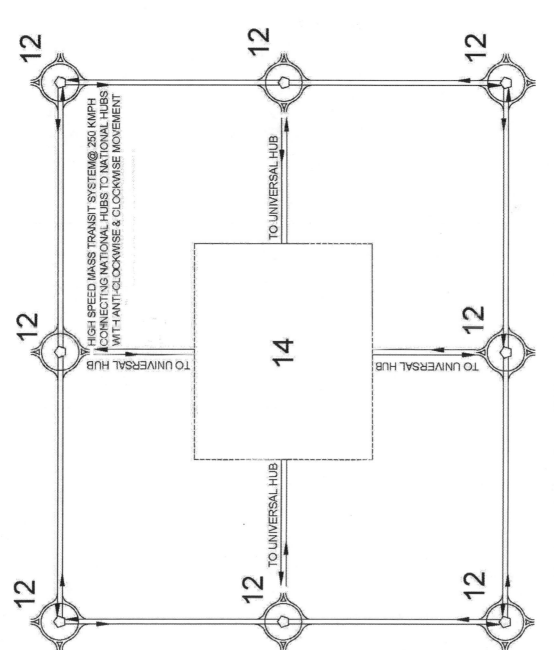

HIGH SPEED MASS TRANSIT SYSTEM@ 250 KMPH
(CONNECTING NATIONAL HUBS TO NATIONAL HUBS
WIT-T ANTI-CLOCKWISE & CLOCKWISE MOVEMENT

TO UNIVERSAL HUB

TO UNIVERSAL HUB

TO UNIVERSAL HUB

TO UNIVERSAL HUB

14

AN EXAMPLE OF HIGH SPEED UNIVERSAL MASS SYSTEM WITHIN THE
PROPOSED METHOD OF HUMAN SETTLEMENT AND URBANIZATION

FIG   11A

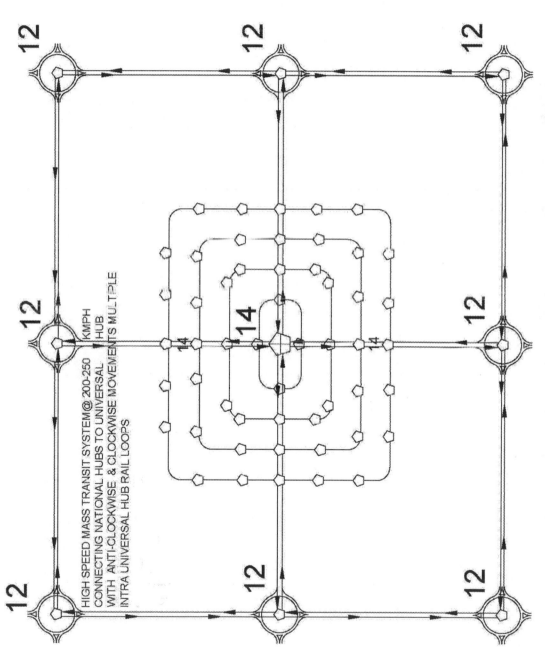

12 12 12

12 12

12 12 12

14 14 14 14

KMPH
HUB

HIGH SPEED MASS TRANSIT SYSTEM@ 200-250
CONNECTING NATIONAL HUBS TO UNIVERSAL
WITH ANTI-CLOCKWISE & CLOCKWISE MOVEMENTS MULTIPLE
INTRA UNIVERSAL HUB RAIL LOOPS

AN EXAMPLE OF HIGH SPEED UNIVERSAL MASS TRANSIT SYSTEM
WITHIN THE PROPOSED METHOD OF HUMAN SETTLEMENT AND URBANIZATION

FIG   11B

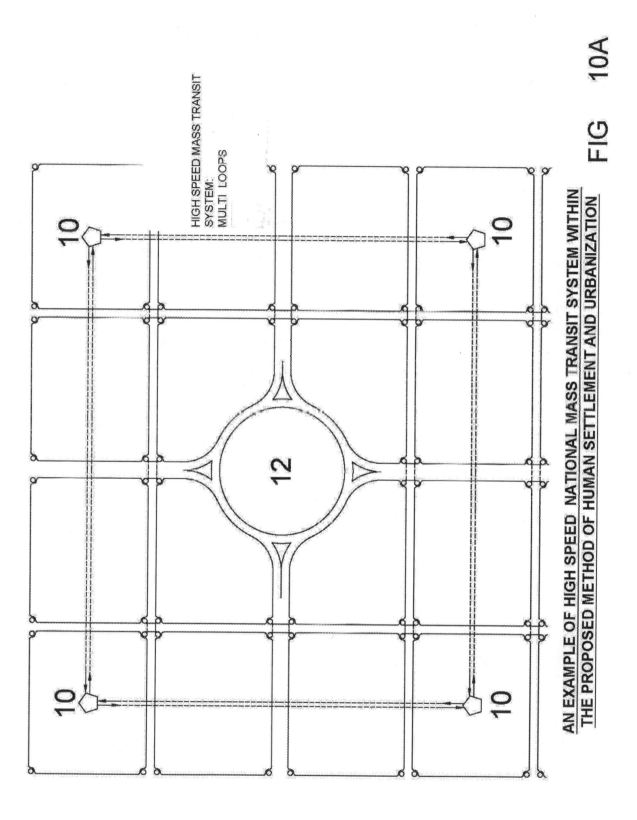

HIGH SPEED MASS TRANSIT
SYSTEM:
MULTI LOOPS

10

10

12

10

10

AN EXAMPLE OF HIGH SPEED NATIONAL MASS TRANSIT SYSTEM WITHIN
THE PROPOSED METHOD OF HUMAN SETTLEMENT AND URBANIZATION

FIG   10A

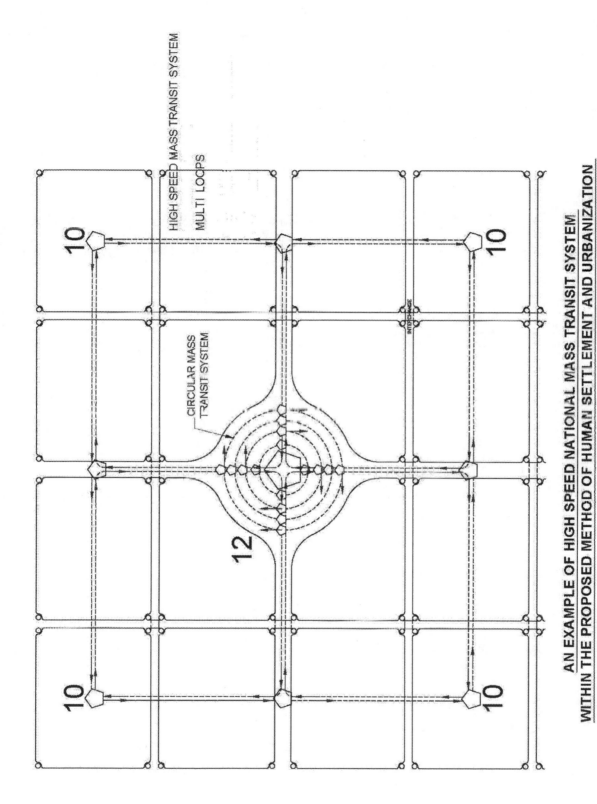

HIGH SPEED MASS TRANSIT SYSTEM

MULTI LOOPS

CIRCULAR MASS
TRANSIT SYSTEM

INTERCHANGE

10

10

10

10

12

AN EXAMPLE OF HIGH SPEED NATIONAL MASS TRANSIT SYSTEM
WITHIN THE PROPOSED METHOD OF HUMAN SETTLEMENT AND URBANIZATION

FIG   10B

High speed Indusrails **24** are developed connecting Industrial Hubs **10s** with each other within their respective National Stratum or Domain **13**; with the Industrial Hubs **10s** of their immediate National Strata **13s** only; and with the National Hubs **12s** of their respective National Stratum or Domain **13** with intermittent stops only at the Hubs and at intersection points with Unirails **26**, Nationrails **25** and Sociorails **23** in a series or parallel loop clockwise or (and) anticlockwise or (and) in a Back-Forth fashion between 2 Industrial Hubs **10**. The speed limit should be around 200 Kmph. The railcar may make more than 1 stop within a hub. An example is as shown in FIG 10a and FIG 10b. An example of the Indusrails is shown in FIG 10A and FIG 10B. This may also be given name based on their level as Level-2 Transit

High speed Sociorails **23** connecting Social Hubs **8s** with each other within their respective Industrial Stratum or Domain **11** with the Social Hubs **8s** of their immediate Industrial Strata **11s** only; and with the Industrial Hubs **10** of their respective Industrial Stratum or Domain **11** with intermittent stops only at the Hubs and at intersection points with Unirails **26**, Nationrails **25** and Indusrails **24** in a series or (and) parallel loop clockwise or anticlockwise or (and) in a Back-Forth fashion between 2 Social Hubs **8s.** The speed limit should be around 125 Kmph. The railcar may make more than 1 stop within a hub. An example of the Sociorails is shown in FIG 9A and FIG 9B. This may also be given name based on their level as Level-1 Transit

Within a Social Stratum or Domain **9s** as shown in FIG 8A and FIG 8B, the high speed bus system is developed such that, though they do not enter the Neighborhood Strata **5s**, they run along the periphery of Neighborhood Strata **5s** within a Community Stratum or Domain **7s** connecting the Neighborhood Strata **5s** to each other and to the Community Hubs **6s** and Social Hub **8s** of the respective Social Stratum or Domain **9**. These buses may have stops as shown in the FIG 8A and FIG 8B, as these buses connects the Socioways **19**, run in completely separate lanes along the Sociaways **19** with no connection with the Socioways **19** around a Community Stratum or Domain **7** except those directed towards the Social Hubs **8s**

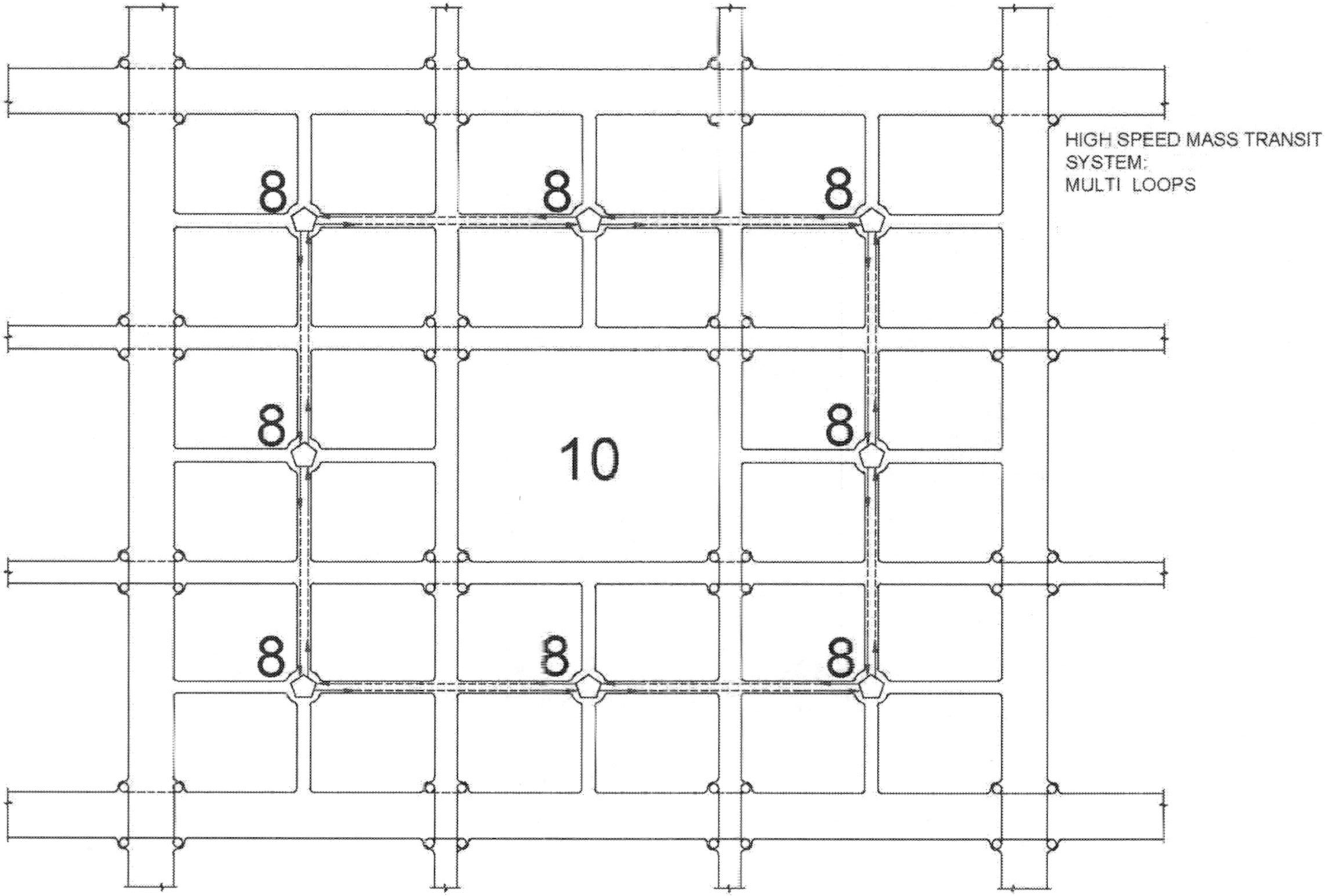

HIGH SPEED MASS TRANSIT
SYSTEM:
MULTI LOOPS

8

8

8

8

10

8

8

8

8

AN EXAMPLE OF HIGH SPEED INDUSTRIAL MASS TRANSIT SYSTEM WITHIN THE
PROPOSED METHOD OF HUMAN SETTLEMENT AND URBANIZATION

FIG 9A

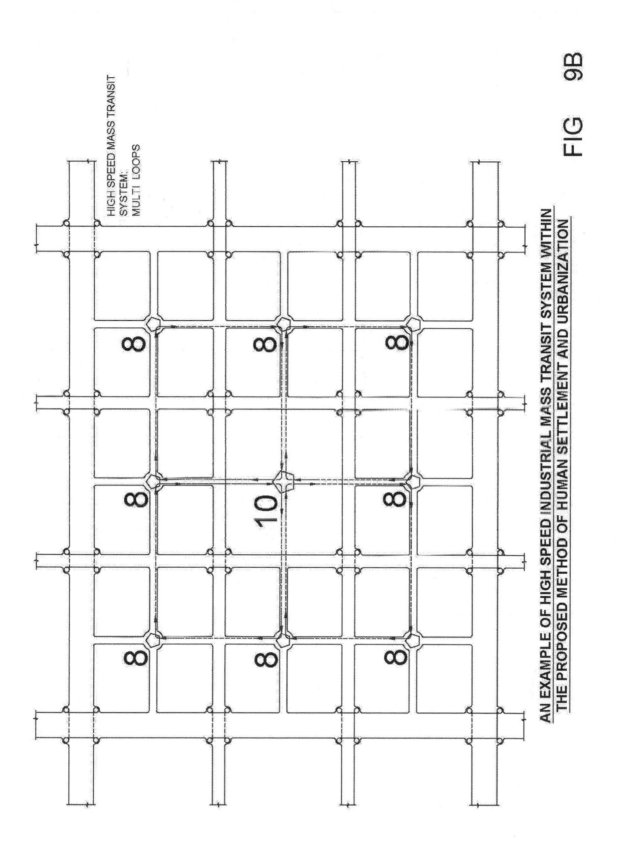

HIGH SPEED MASS TRANSIT
SYSTEM:
MULTI LOOPS

8

8

8

8

10

8

8

8

8

AN EXAMPLE OF HIGH SPEED INDUSTRIAL MASS TRANSIT SYSTEM WITHIN
THE PROPOSED METHOD OF HUMAN SETTLEMENT AND URBANIZATION

FIG 9B

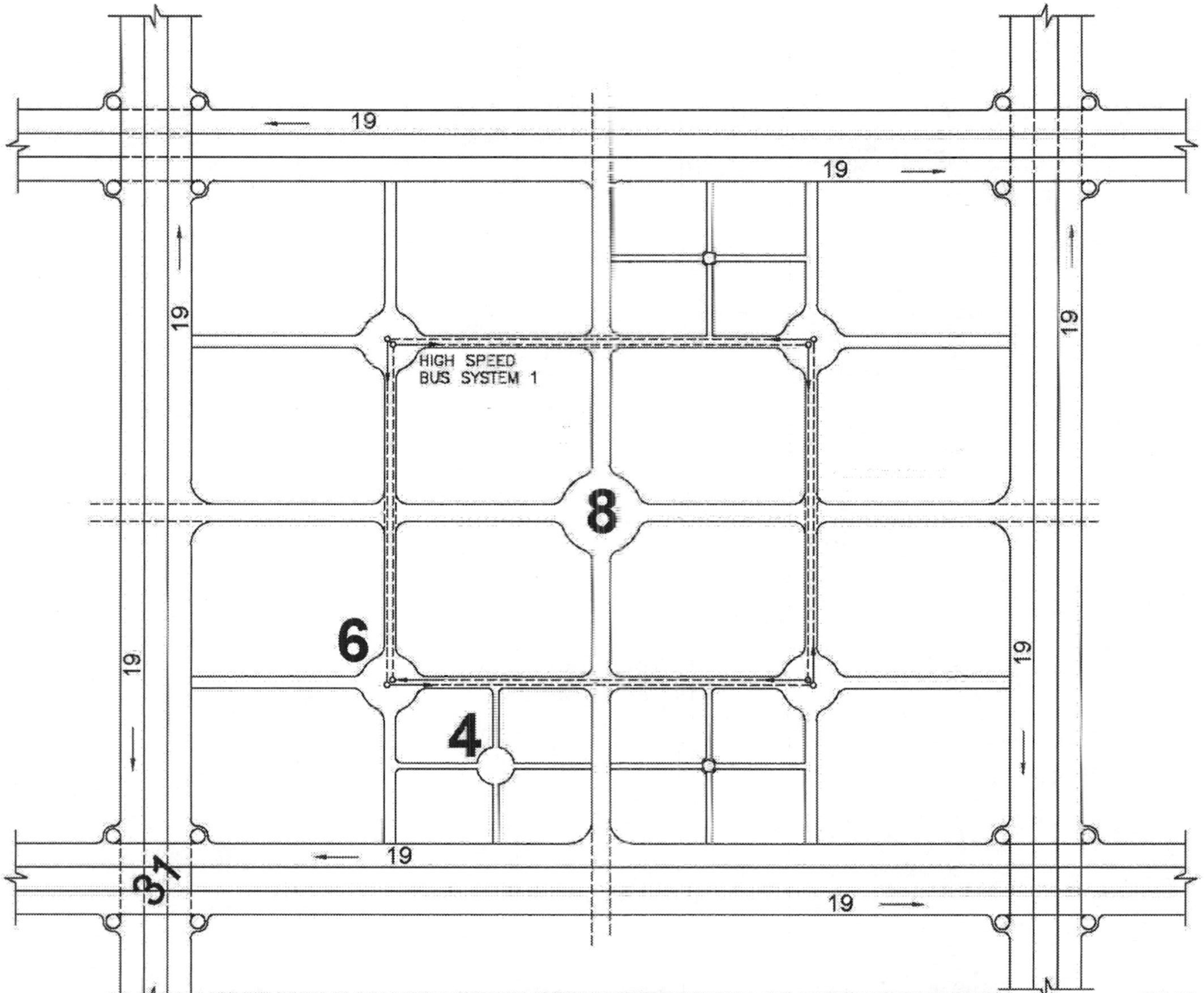

HIGH SPEED
BUS SYSTEM 1

AN EXAMPLE OF HIGH SPEED COMMUNITY-SOCIAL TRANSPORT SYSTEM
WITHIN THE PROPOSED METHOD OF HUMAN SETTLEMENT AND URBANIZATION

FIG 8A

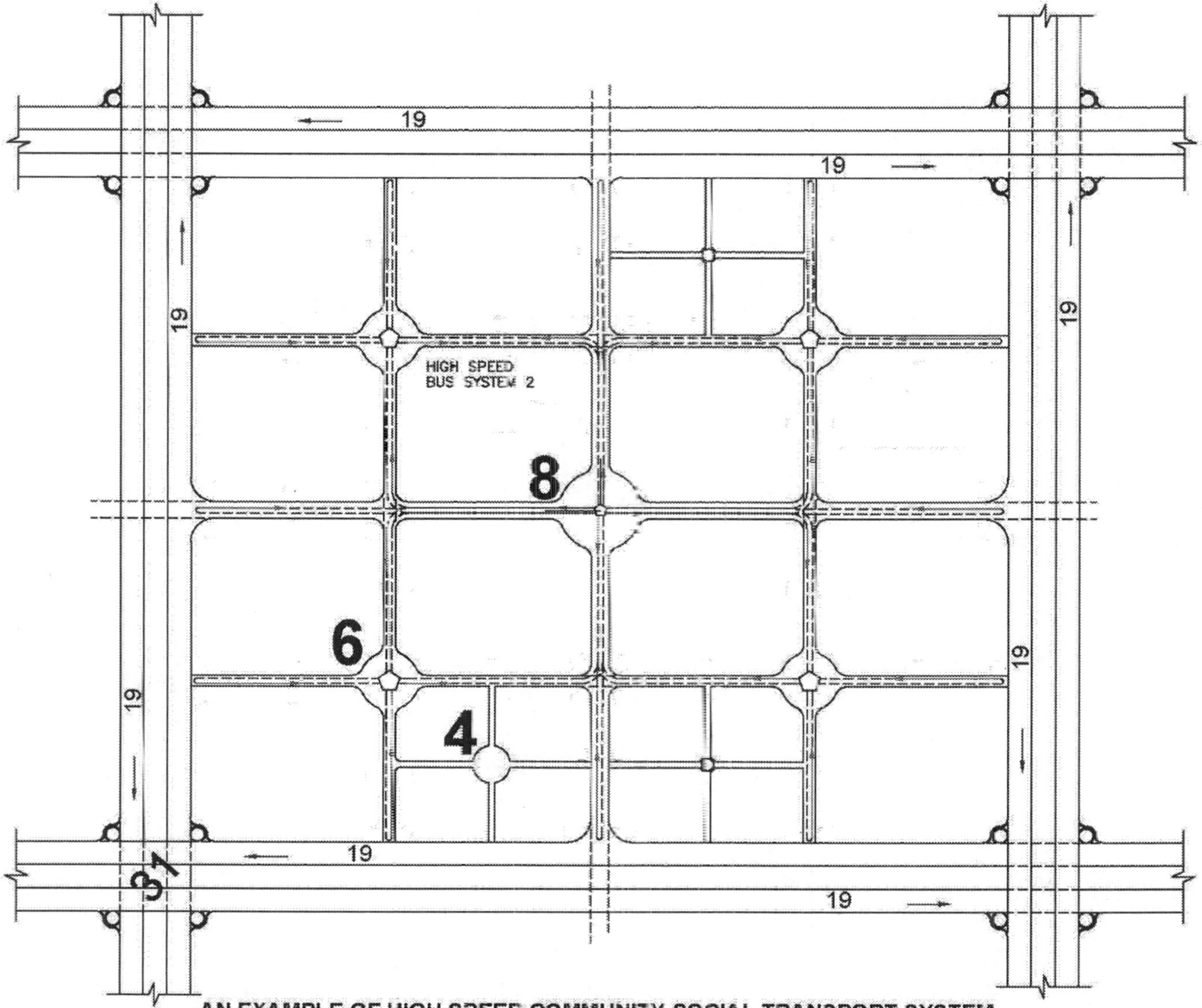

HIGH SPEED
BUS SYSTEM 2

8

4

6

19

19

19

19

19

19

19

19

AN EXAMPLE OF HIGH SPEED COMMUNITY-SOCIAL TRANSPORT SYSTEM
WITHIN THE PROPOSED METHOD OF HUMAN SETTLEMENT AND URBANIZATION

FIG 8B

HARMONIC FLYWAYS SYSTEM:

An urban planning is successful only if most of its aspects would continue to be robust and valid in all ages and is capable of accommodating the future aspects and requirements of a human dwelling and society. Development of Harmonic Flyways System for flying vehicles in the proposed urban system is going to be such an approach. These flyways must be classified into levels according to their designated altitudes and in order to keep such flying vehicles away from residential and primary or elementary schooling areas, so that private family and neighborhood living may not be disturbed by such future aspects of transportation, this flyways system starts at its lowest level from Community Hubs **6s**. Furthermore in the proposed human settlements and urban development, such system of flyways connects only the hubs and flies over the roadways only. In this system of transportation there are corridors in space above the ground level connecting the hubs with respectively same social energy level hubs and corresponding lower or higher social energy level hubs in space such that altitude of corridors with destination at the hubs with lower social activity energy level are lower as compared to the altitude of corridors with destination at the hubs with comparatively higher social energy activity level etc

There are following governing rules and principles for flyways related to hubs:

The Community Hubs **6s** are connected with each other and corresponding higher level hubs through this system of Line-1 of Harmonic Flyways System only in a straight line and directly over the Harmonic Roadways System at the lowest possible altitude and must not fly over any building accommodating human beings. All the flying vehicles designated for this hub fly at the Line-1 assigned altitude, irrespective of the hub from where the journey is to be initiated. Specific areas should be designated within hubs for these flying vehicles and may be called as Flypads. The speed limit for this corridor is going to be the lowest

The Social Hubs **8s** are connected with each other and corresponding lower and higher level hubs through this system of Line-2 of Harmonic Flyways System only in a straight line and directly over the Harmonic Roadways System at the lowest possible altitude but higher than Line--1 altitude, and must not fly over any building accommodating human beings. All the flying vehicles designated for this hub fly at the Line-2 assigned altitude irrespective of the hub from where the journey is to be initiated. Specific areas should be designated within hubs for these flying vehicles and may be called as Flypads. The speed limit for this corridor is going to be higher than Corridor Line-1 but lower than other levels

The Industrial Hubs **10s** are connected with each other and corresponding lower and higher level hubs through this system of Line-3 of Harmonic Flyways System only in a straight line and directly over the Harmonic Roadways System at the lowest possible altitude but higher than Line 1 and Line 2 altitude, and must not fly over any building accommodating human beings. All the flying vehicles designated for this hub fly at the Line 3 assigned altitude irrespective of the hub from where the journey is to be initiated. Specific areas should be designated within hubs for these flying vehicles and may be called as Flypads. The speed limit for this corridor is going to be higher than Corridor Line 1 and Line 2 but lower than other levels

The National Hubs **12s** are connected with each other and corresponding lower and higher level hubs through this system of Line 4 of Harmonic Flyways System only in a straight line and directly over the Harmonic Roadways System at the lowest possible altitude but higher than Line 1, Line 2 and Line 3 altitude, and must not fly over any building accommodating human beings. All the flying vehicles designated for this hub fly at the Line 4 assigned altitude irrespective of the hub from where the journey is to be initiated. Specific areas should be designated within hubs for these flying vehicles and may be called as Flypads. The speed limit for this corridor is going to be higher than Corridor Line 1, Line 2 and Line 3 but lower than other Lines

The Universal Hubs **14s** are connected with each other and corresponding lower level hubs through this system of Line 5 of Harmonic Flyways System only in a straight line and directly over Harmonic Roadways System at lowest possible altitude but higher than Line 1, Line 2, Line 3 and Line 4 altitude, and must not fly over any building accommodating human beings. All the flying vehicles designated for this hub fly at the Line 5 assigned altitude irrespective of the hub from where the journey is to be initiated. Specific areas should be designated within hubs for these flying vehicles and may be called as Flypads. The speed limit for this corridor is going to be higher than Corridor Line 1, Line 2, Line 3 and Line 4

FORMULATION OF THE PRINCIPLES

1. A method or procedure for the development of human settlement and urbanization, comprising:
    a) Identifying and classifying human social activities based on types and levels of social activity energy;
    b) Developing human social activity hubs; and
    c) Allocating the classified human social activities to the human social activity hubs developed as mentioned above

2. As per the method or procedure 1, wherein developing human social activity hubs further comprises identifying the human social activity hubs as Private Hubs, Neighborhood Hubs, Community Hubs, Social Hubs, Industrial Hubs, National Hubs, Universal Hubs and may be Agrarian Hubs based on the order of social activity types and relative human social activity energy levels

3. As per the method or procedure 1, further comprising:
    Building or creation of residential units around the social activity hubs with lower most human social activity energy levels or (and) logically related social activity types, to be designated as Private Hubs and are considered as the basic building blocks or cells or entity of proposed human settlement urban setup and are hereby called Family Cells

4. As per the clause 3, further comprising: The development and linking of more than 1 Family Cells with the same or variable sizes and shapes approximately at equal intervals of space to create a comparatively lower human social activity stratum or domain called Private Stratum or Domain

5. As per the clause 1, further comprising; The development of more than one Private Strata with the same or variable sizes and shapes approximately at equal

intervals of space around a human social activity hub with comparatively higher social activity energy levels than Private Hub or (and) logically related unique social activity types, hereby may be called as Neighborhood Hub, to create a comparatively higher human social activity Stratum or Domain hereby called Neighborhood Stratum or Domain

6. As per the clause 1, further comprising; The development of more than one Neighborhood Strata with the same or variable sizes and shapes approximately at equal intervals of space around a human social activity hub with comparatively higher social activity energy levels than Neighborhood Hub or (and) logically related unique social activity types, hereby may be called as Community Hub, to create a comparatively higher human social activity Stratum or Domain hereby called Community Stratum or Domain

7. As per the clause 1, further comprising; The development of more than one Community Strata with the same or variable sizes and shapes approximately at equal intervals of space around a human social activity hub with comparatively higher social activity energy levels than Community Hub or (and) logically related unique social activity types, hereby may be called as Social Hub, to create a comparatively higher human social activity Stratum or Domain hereby called Social Stratum or Domain

8. As per the clause 1, further comprising; The development of more than one Social Strata with the same or variable sizes and shapes approximately at equal intervals of space around a human social activity hub with comparatively higher social activity energy levels than Social Hub or (and) logically related unique social activity types, hereby may be called as Industrial Hub, to create a comparatively higher human social activity Stratum or Domain hereby called Industrial Stratum or Domain

9. As per the clause 1, further comprising: The development of more than one Industrial Strata with the same or variable sizes and shapes approximately at equal intervals of space around a human social activity hub with comparatively higher social activity energy levels than Industrial Hub or (and) logically related unique social activity types, hereby may be called as National Hub, to create a comparatively higher human social activity stratum or domain hereby called National Stratum or Domain

10. As per the clause 1, further comprising: The development of more than one National Strata with the same or variable sizes and shapes approximately at equal intervals of space around a human social activity hub with comparatively

higher social activity energy levels than National Hub or (and) logically related unique social activity types, hereby may be called as Universal Hub, to create a comparatively higher human social activity stratum or domain called Universal Stratum or Domain and vice versa hence simulating a galaxy

11. As per the clause 1, such that the proposed human social activity hubs though may not exactly, but are located approximately at the center of their respective Strata

12. As per the clause 1, such that any two of the hubs as mentioned above may be combined to form a hybrid stratum or domain or any of the hubs may split into further classified strata as per the requirements and other constraints which may arise from time to time, geography to geography and society to society

13. A method or procedure of developing roadways system hereby called as Harmonic Roadways System (HRS), such that these roadways are connecting hubs classified with the same or different social activity energy levels or (and) types of social activities within Intra-Universal-Stratum or Domain or (and) Inter-Universal-Stratum or Domain level, without any kind of stops or (and) traffic signals such that these roadways have exit and entramps for vehicles only at hubs and at intersecting points with other roadways of same or (and) different levels and may be classified as Privways or HRS Level-1, Neighborways or HRS Level-2, Commways or HRS Level-3, Socioways or HRS Level-4, Indusways or HRS Level-5, Nationways or HRS Level-6 and Uniways or HRS Level-7 etc based on levels or (and) types of hubs they are primarily related to

14. As per the clause 13, further comprising:
Development of Uniways or HRS Level-7 with tracks of maximum possible and logical speed limits for land as well as flying vehicles linking or connecting Universal Hubs with each other or (and) other consecutive lower and higher level hubs through Exit-Entrance ramps and with corresponding intersecting Uniways or HRS Level-7, Nationways or HRS Level-6 and the Indusways or HRS Level-5 through interchanges at the Uniways-Uniways or HRS Level-7--Level-7, the Uniways-Nationways or HRS Level-7--Level-6 and Uniways-Indusways or HRS Level-7--Level-5 intersections respectively

15. As per the clause 13, further comprising:
Development of Nationways or HRS Level-6 with tracks of maximum possible and logical speed limit, for land as well as flying vehicles, linking or

connecting National Hubs with each other or (and) other consecutive lower and higher level hubs through Exit-Entrance ramps and with corresponding intersecting Uniways or HRS Level-7, Nationways or HRS Level-6, Indusways or HRS Level-5 and the Socioways or HRS Level-4 through interchanges at the Nationways-Uniways or HRS Level-6--Level-7, Nationways-Nationways or HRS Level-6--Level-6, Nationways-Indusways or HRS Level-6--Level-5 and Nationways-Socioways or HRS Level-6--Level-4 intersections

16. As per the clause 13, further comprising:

Development of Indusways with tracks of maximum possible speed limit, for land as well as flying vehicles, linking or connecting Industrial Hubs with each other or (and) other consecutive lower and higher level hubs through Exit-Entrance ramps and with corresponding intersecting Uniways or HRS Level-7, Nationways or HRS Level-6, Indusways or HRS Level-5 and the Socioways or HRS Level-4 through interchanges at the Indusways-Uniways or HRS Level-5--Level-7, Indusways-Nationways or HRS Level-5--Level-6, Indusways-Indusways or HRS Level-5--Level-5 and Indusways-Socioways or HRS Level-5--Level-4 intersections

17. As per the clause 13, further comprising:

Development of Socioways linking or connecting Social Hubs with each other within the same Universal Stratum or Domain and other consecutive lower and higher level hubs through Exit-Entrance ramps and with corresponding intersecting Nationways or HRS Level-6, Indusways or HRS Level-5, Socioways or HRS Level-4 and the Commways or HRS Level-3 through interchanges at Socioways-Nationways or HRS Level-4--Level-6, Socioways-Indusways or HRS Level-4--Level-5, Socioways-Socioways or HRS Level-4--Level-4 and the Socioways-Commways or HRS Level-4--Level-3 intersections

18. As per the clause 13, further comprising:

Development of Commways linking or connecting Community Hubs with each other within their respective Social Stratum or Domain and other consecutive lower and higher level hubs with corresponding intersecting Neighborways or HRS Level-2 and Socioways or HRS Level-4 through interchanges at the Commways-Socioways or HRS Level-3--Level-4 and Commways-Neighborways or HRS Level-3--Level-2 intersections within their respective Social Stratum or Domain

19. As per the clause 13, further comprising:

Development of Neighborways or HRS Level-2 linking or connecting Neighborhood Hubs with each other within their respective Community Stratum or Domain and other consecutive lower and higher level hubs with corresponding intersecting Commways or HRS Level-3 and Privways or HRS Level-1through interchanges at the Neighborways-Commways or HRS Level-2--Level-3 and Neighborways-Privways or HRS Level-2--Level-1 intersections

20. As per the clause 13, further comprising:

    Development of Privways or HRS Level-linking or connecting Private Hubs to each other within their respective Neighborhood Stratum or Domain and the Neighborways or HRS Level-2 surrounding the respective Private Strata

21. The method or procedure of developing a railways system hereby may be called as Harmonic Railways System such that these high speed railways are connecting hubs with the same social activity energy levels or types to each other and to their corresponding hubs with lower or higher social activity energy levels or types, in clockwise or anti-clockwise loops or in a line, within the Inter-Universal-Stratum or Domain or (and) Intra-Universal-Stratum or Domain level, without any kind of intermittent stop such that the corresponding railcars have stops only at hubs and at intersecting points with other railways of same level or (and) with the following lower or (and) higher level(s). These railways may be called as Sociorails or Rail-1, Indusrails or Rail-2, Nationrails or Rail-3 and Unirails or Rail-4 etc according to their respective hubs they are linking

22. The method or procedure of developing a flyways system hereby may be called as Harmonic Flyways System for flying vehicles in the proposed urban system with their landing pads located only within the classified Hubs except Private Hubs and the Neighborhood Hubs such that there are corridors in space directly above the Harmonic Roadways System in a line with levels designated according to their destination Hubs and regardless of their originating Hubs ranging from lowest safest altitude for the Community Hubs as destination to the respectively highest safest altitude for the Universal Hubs as destination thus connecting the various Hubs within the proposed human settlement urban development. These Flyways may be called as Socioline or Line-1, Indusline or Line-2, Nationline or Line-3 and Uniline or Line-4 etc according to their respective hubs they are linking primarily as their destination

REFERENCES

1. Abbott, Carl. "Urban History for Planners," Journal of Planning History, Nov 2006, Vol. 5 Issue 4

2. Engeli, Christian, and Horst Matzerath. Modern Urban History Research in Europe, USA, and Japan: a handbook (1989)

3. Goldfield, David. ed. Encyclopedia of American Urban History (2 vol 2006)

4. Hays, Samuel P. "From the History of the City to the History of the Urbanized Society," Journal of Urban History, (1993)

5. Reulecke, Jürgen; Huck, Gerhard; Sutcliffe, Anthony. "Urban History Research in Germany: Its Development and Present Condition," Urban History Yearbook 1981

6. Sahlins M.D, Evolution and Culture, University of Michigan Press, 1970

7. Graber, Robert B., A Scientific Model of Social and Cultural Evolution, 1995, Thomas Jefferson University Press, Kirksville, MO

8. Hatch, Elvin, Theories of Man and Culture, 1973, Columbia Univ Press

9. Johnson, Allen W. and Earle, Timothy, The Evolution of Human Societies: From Foraging Group to Agrarian State, 1987, Stanford University Press

10. Eisenstadt, SN (1973). Tradition, Change, and Modernity. Krieger Publishing

11. McMillan W, Chavis M, Sense of Community: A Definition and Theory, 1986

12. What Do Planners Do? Power, Politics, and Persuasion, Charles Hoch, American Planning Association, 1994. ISBN 978-0-918286-91-8

13. "The City Shaped: Urban Patterns and Meanings Through History", Spiro Kostof, 2nd Edition, Thames and Hudson Ltd, 1999 ISBN 978-0-500-28099-7

14. Jackson, Peter and Susan J. Smith (1984): Exploring Social Geography. Boston, London (Allen & Unwin)

15. Valentine, Gill (2001): Social Geographies: Space and Society. New York (Prentice Hall) Gregory, Derek and John Urry (eds.) (1985): Social Relations and Spatial Structures. Basingstoke et al. (MacMillan)
16. Werlen, Benno (1993): Society, Action and Space: An Alternative Human Geography. London, New York (Routledge)
17. Forbes, Scott, A Natural History of Families, Princeton Univ Press, 2005
18. Katz, Peter (1994). The New Urbanism: Toward An Architecture of Community NY McGraw-Hill
19. Planning for Soviet Union, Judith Pallot & Denis J.B. Shaw,1981
20. Tönnies, Ferdinand (1887). *Gemeinschaft und Gesellschaft*, (Translated, 1957 by Charles P. Loomis as *Community and Society*, East Lansing MSU Press)